Contents

WAIS
AND
GOPHER
SERVERS

A Guide for
Internet End-Users

ERIC LEASE MORGAN

Mecklermedia
Westport • London

Library of Congress Cataloging-in-Publication Data

Morgan, Eric Lease.
    WAIS and Gopher servers : a guide for Internet endusers / Eric
Lease Morgan.
       p. cm.
    Includes bibliographical references and index.
    ISBN 0-88736-932-4 : $
    1. Client/server computing. 2. End-user computing. 3. Internet
(Computer network) I. Title.
QA76.9.C55M67 1994
025.04–dc20   94-12260
                                                    CIP

British Library Cataloguing-in-Publication Data

Morgan, Eric Lease
    WAIS and Gopher Servers: Guide for
    Internet End-users
    I. Title
    004.6

    ISBN 0-88736-932-4

Mecklermedia Corporation, 20 Ketchum Street, Westport, CT 06880.
Mecklermedia Ltd., Artillery House, Artillery Row, London SW1P 1RT, U.K.

Printed on acid free paper.
Printed and bound in the United States of America.

Introduction

This book is a tutorial on the use of WAIS and Gopher. It describes how to use a few WAIS and Gopher clients for DOS, Macintosh, and Unix computers. It also describes how WAIS and Gopher servers can be used to enhance library service.

First, I will describe the client/server model and provide an overview of the WAIS and Gopher protocols in chapter 1.

Chapters 2 through 7 describe how to use various WAIS and Gopher client software for DOS, Macintosh, and Unix computers. Chapter 8 describes how to use veronica. Chapter 9 describes how to create WAIS and Gopher servers on a Unix computer.

Finally, chapters 10 and 11 describe various Gopher server tools used to provide enhanced library service.

This book is intended to be used in conjunction with a particular Gopher server, the Gopher at the NCSU Libraries, but this is not necessary. Follow the instructions in the book; the examples will become more apparent, and you will get a better understanding of what is happening.

In many cases, the book refers to external texts, scripts, or files. All of these resources can be retrieved from the Gopher at the NCSU Libraries in a directory named "Finding Your WAIS Through a Gopher Hole." (From here on out this directory will be called the Finding directory.)

If you already have a Gopher client installed, then here is how to navigate to the Finding directory. Direct your Gopher client to dewey.lib.ncsu.edu on port 70. You will be presented with a list of menus from which you should select the following choices:

1. NCSU's "Library Without Walls",
2. The Stacks, and
3. Finding Your WAIS Through a Gopher Hole.

If you don't have a Gopher client installed, then go to either chapter 3, 5, or 7, depending on whether you are using DOS, a Unix, or a Macintosh computer, to learn how to install a Gopher client.

Alternatively, most of the external texts, scripts, or files are also available via anonymous FTP. In these cases, the resources' locations are described with the use of a brand-new, not-quite-formalized standard called universal resource locators (URL). The purpose of URLs is to present you with an unambiguous description of the location of an item on the Internet. These items can be Gopher items, FTP files, WAIS indexes, and so forth. The vast majority of the URLs listed here are FTP files. Here is your first URL:

```
file://dewey.lib.ncsu.edu/pub/stacks/finding/url.txt
```

This string says:

```
¿ ftp to dewey.lib.ncsu.edu,
¡ log on as anonymous,
¬ send your email address as your password,
√ change directories to /pub/stacks/finding, and
ƒ get the file url.txt.
```

For more information about URLs read Tim Berners-Lee's "Uniform Resource Locators."[1]

A small disclaimer is needed here. Like all computing environments, WAIS and Gopher services are in a constant state of flux. One day a service might appear, and the next day it's gone. One day a service might be located at one particular address, and the next day its address has changed. This is one of the mixed blessings of the Internet, and therefore of WAIS and Gopher. Since there is no central authority governing the creation and maintenance of these services, services can be implemented very quickly. They disappear just as quickly. As you explore the Internet you will come to appreciate, tolerate, and dislike this lack of a central governing authority.

WAIS and Gopher are only a small part of the expanding Internet. As a librarian I find the Internet a very exciting "place."

When I was younger, the library was my window on the world. I could travel anywhere I wanted simply by finding the right book. Now I don't even have to go to the library to do this. I can travel all over the world simply by sitting down at my computer.

In addition to serving as a tutorial, this book has another purpose. It is my intention to instill into you the same excitement I feel for exploring and learning. The computer is a marvelous tool, but that is all it is, a tool. It has given me access to information all over the world. It allows me to communicate with people from distant lands. More importantly, the computer has allowed me to create information tools and services for other people so they can do the same. This book is just another means to those ends.

Eric Lease Morgan
Systems Librarian
North Carolina State University
Raleigh, North Carolina

Note

1. URL=file://dewey.lib.ncsu.edu/pub/stacks/finding/url.txt

1

An Overview of WAIS and Gopher

This chapter provides an overview of WAIS and Gopher. It does so first by describing the client/server model of computing. Then it demonstrates how WAIS and Gopher use this model.

If you simply want to learn how to use your client software, then skip this chapter. On the other hand, if you want to know a bit about what is going on behind the scenes or you don't want to lose your orientation in WAISspace and Gopherspace, then this chapter is for you.

The Client/Server Model

In a sentence, the client/server model is a form of distributed computing in which one program, the client, communicates with another program, the server, for the purpose of exchanging information. Within this model, various aspects of a computing task (typically a database search) are divided between at least two programs, the client and the server.

The client is primarily responsible for

- the user interface,
- initiating the communications process, and
- interpreting any information sent from the server.

On the other hand, the server's primary purposes are to

- analyze any communications from the client,
- perform any computations because of those communications, and
- return to the client the information resulting from the computations.

Put another way, client/server computing provides a mechanism for disparate computers to cooperate on a single computing task.

User-interface development is the most obvious advantage in client/server computing. Within this model it is possible to create an interface to data independent of the computing environment hosting the data. For instance, the user interface of a client/server application can be written on a Macintosh and the server can be written on a mainframe. At the same time, clients written for DOS- or Unix-based computers could access the same data from the same mainframe. Since the user interface is now the responsibility of the client, the server has more computing resources to spend on analyzing any queries and disseminating information. Here lies another advantage of client/server computing; it tends to use the strengths of divergent computing platforms to create more powerful applications. There is no reason why a Macintosh could not be used as a server, but its computing and storage capabilities are dwarfed by the mainframe's. The client/server model also provides the opportunity to store information in a central location and disseminate that information regardless of what type the remote computer is.

Here is an algorithm outlining a typical client/server interaction:

1. The user runs client software to create a query.
2. The client connects to the server.
3. The client sends the query to the server.
4. The server analyzes the query.
5. The server computes the results of the query.
6. The server sends the results to the client.
7. The client presents the results to the user.
8. Repeat as necessary.

Figure 1-1 illustrates the same interaction.

WAIS

WAIS in an acronym for Wide Area Information Server. Initially, it represented the joint efforts of Thinking Machines, Apple

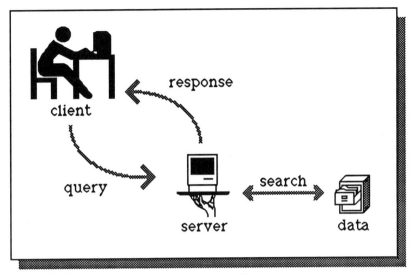

Figure 1-1. A typical client/server interaction.

Computer, and Dow Jones. Introduced in 1991, its purpose was to demonstrate how documents could be stored on a central computer and disseminated to remote computers with the use of a simple user interface.[1]

Using WAIS as an example, this is how the client/server model works: First the user runs a WAIS client program. This program may run on a DOS, Macintosh, Unix, or any other computing platform. Using the client software, the user forms a query specifying a database(s) to search and the search terms. Once the query is created, the client initiates communications to the user-specified server(s) and transmits the query. The server then interprets the query and applies it against its data. After the result of the query is obtained, the result is sent back to the client. Now the client interprets the response and reformats it for the user. Based on the results presented to the user, the user has the opportunity to create a new query and repeat the process. One of the unique features of the WAIS clients is their ability to query many databases (servers) simultaneously. Therefore you could search for the term "sun" in databases with information about astronomy, physics, literature, or lyrics all at the same time. Figure 1-2 illustrates this concept.

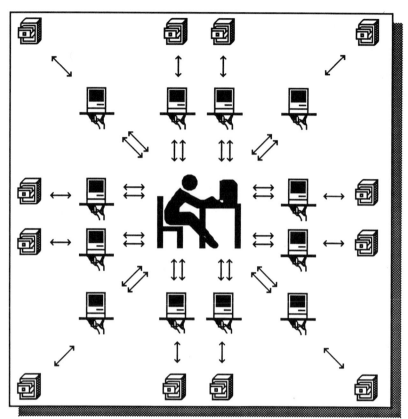

Figure 1-2. The WAIS protocol allows a user to search multiple servers simultaneously.

Another unique feature of WAIS is its ability to rank the retrieved results by relevance. Depending on the server's indexing algorithm, the value of a document is based on the position of a term in a document, the number of times a term is located in a document, the number of times the term appears in the database, and the length of the document. Each of the weighting algorithms of the three (presently) existing versions of the WAIS indexer is explained here.

In the original WAIS distribution, the value of a document is based on an algorithm whereby each document is given a weight determined by the position of a search term(s) in a document and the total number of times the search term(s) is located in a document. Here is a paragraph from the source code describing this idea:

The [WAIS] indexer is a very simple inverted file system with primitive word weighting. What is created is an inverted index of all the words over 2 characters long in the input text. Words are truncated to 20 characters. Each word has [a] weight associated with it; the first time it occurs in a document it gets an extra weight of 5, and from then on, it gets a weight of 1 in that document. Words in the headline are worth an extra 10. Searching is done by finding the documents with the most word weights for each word in the query. Relevant documents' words are worth 10 times less.

This algorithm is listed below:

1. If the search term occurs in the body of a document, then the document is given a weight of 5 (W).
2. Add 1 to W for each additional time the search term occurs in the body of the document.
3. Add 10 to W if the search term occurs in the headline (usually the first line) of the document.
4. If W >= 127 then W = 127.
5. Calculate W for each document that contains the search term(s).
6. Assign a rank of 1000 to the document with the highest weight (W).
7. Rank every other document with a W > 0 by proportionally normalizing them with the highest ranking document.

Since the original WAIS distribution did not include Boolean operations, a nasty wrench gets thrown into the works when you supply more than one term in the query. For example, if you searched a WAIS index (compiled by the original WAIS distribution) with the query "dogs and cats," then the server will look for the terms "dogs," "and," and "cats." This probably isn't what you want. Furthermore, there may exist a document that contains the word "dog" 1000 times but does not contain the word "cat." At the same time there may exist a document that contains the word "dog" 250 times and the word "cat" 250 times. If this were true, then the first document would be considered more relevant than the second document. Obviously, traditional

WAIS indexes are better suited for single-term queries. This is not so bad, considering that many people use only single-term queries at the outset anyway.

Since the original WAIS distribution was released by Thinking Machines, Don Gilbert of Indiana University added Boolean searching to the algorithm. This distribution, frequently called IUBio,[2] first applied the Boolean operations to the database and then applied the weighting scheme from the original distribution to the resulting set.

Next, Jim Fullton of the Clearinghouse for Networked Information Discovery and Retrieval (CNIDR) completed and released freeWAIS[3] which includes not only Boolean searching and stemming but also the use of a thesaurus and an enhanced document-ranking algorithm. This distribution is a bit more intelligent in that it takes into account the number of times a term is located in the entire database as well as the length of the document. This algorithm can be expressed algebraically:

$$[10 + \log (B + H) / E] / L = W$$

where

$B =$ the number of times a search term is found in the body of the document;

$H =$ the number of times a search term is found in the headline, multiplied by 5;

$E =$ the number of times a search term is found in the entire database;

$L =$ the length of the document measured in characters; and

$W =$ the weight of a document.

After each document is assigned a weight, the highest-ranking document is given a score of 1000, and every other document with a $W > 0$ is proportionally normalized. This normalization process is the same as that in the last step of the original distribution.

Here is an example of how relevance works. There is a WAIS server distributing the texts of USENET frequently asked questions (FAQ).[4] The server is located on a computer named "pit-manager.mit.edu" on port 210. (A port is a communications point. Think of it as a telephone number extension.) The database is called "usenetfaq.src". When you send the WAIS-generated query "Gopher" to pit-manager.mit.edu, the server searches for documents with the word "Gopher." This list of documents is returned to the client software. The documents with higher scores are presented higher in the list. The documents with lower scores are returned and presented lower in the list. Below are the first ten titles returned from such a query:

```
gopher@boo Re: Gopher (comp.infosystems.gopher) Frequently Asked Q...
kristoff@n Re: BIOSCI/bionet Frequently Asked Questions.
ilana@kiow Re: Sources of Meteorological Data FAQ.
smith-una@ Re: A Biologist's Guide to Internet Resources (FAQ).
TeXhax-Req Re: TeXhax Digest V93 #004.
kaminski@n Re: Public Dialup Internet Access List (PDIAL).
jik@athena Re: FAQ: How to find people's E-mail addresses.
yanoff@csd Re: Updated Internet Services List.
dalamb@quc Re: FAQ: College Email Addresses 3/3 [Monthly posting].
agbrooks@t Re: rec.pyrotechnics FAQ.
```

The first item in the list is indeed an FAQ about Gopher. The other documents in the list probably contain the word "Gopher" at least once, and therefore they are considered relevant.

The use of specific WAIS clients and the creation of WAIS servers are described in later chapters of the book.

Gopher

The Gopher protocol is also built on the client/server model. Originally developed at the University of Minnesota Microcomputer, Workstation, Networks Center in April 1991, the Internet Gopher has grown from a campus-wide information system to a worldwide information system.

At one time Gopher was described as Internet glue because with one program (a Gopher client) a user can:

- display and save text files,
- automatically run telnet sessions,

- ftp to remote computers,
- do WAIS searches, and
- retrieve multimedia files (sounds, video clips, graphics).

Furthermore, the user doesn't need to remember Internet names, addresses, or commands. All the user has to do is select items from a menu.

In a nutshell, this is how Gopher works. First the user runs a Gopher client. Presently, Gopher clients come in just about every computing platform except the most esoteric. The user's client program is usually configured to "point"[5] to a particular Gopher server. Once the client is run, it sends a query to the designated server and asks for a list of what is available. The server responds accordingly and the client displays the results.[6] Figure 1-3 shows what is displayed when a (Unix curses) Gopher client first points to the Gopher server dewey.lib.ncsu.edu on port 70.

Now the user simply selects items from this menu and presses return. The client then analyzes the type of query represented by the menu items, forms a new query, and sends it back to the server. There are quite a number of different menu types, and they are all described in the chapters on the Gopher clients. Figure 1-4 shows a list of the most common items and how they are indicated on a menu.

When the user selects item 2 from the menu in Figure 1-3, the Gopher client retrieves a text file from the server. If the user

```
-> 1.Welcome!.
   2.A map of this Gopher as of 1/6/93.
   3.Search this Gopher <?>
   4.What's new?.
   5.Happenings!, NCSU's Campus Wide Information Server <TEL>
   6.About the North Carolina State University Libraries/
   7.NCSU's "Library Without Walls"/
   8.Beyond the Libraries /
```

Figure 1-3. The main menu of the gopher named "The Gopher at the NCSU Libraries".

selects item 3, then he or she is prompted for a word to search. This particular search searches for a menu item from this particular server; it is an index to the server, and thus the server will respond with a list of menu items within this server that contain this search term.[7] Similarly, if the user chooses item 7 the server "changes directories" to NCSU's "Library Without Walls" and displays the contents of that directory.

Since the original Gopher protocol was released, many enhancements have been added, including the ability to run remote programs and display graphics. A few Gopher administrators have modified the original distribution to suit their own needs. More important, the Gopher Team at the University of Minnesota has introduced a new Gopher protocol called Gopher+. Gopher+ is supposed to be completely backward compatible with the original Gopher protocol and includes the ability to add data to servers, fill out forms to be sent to particular

Type	Unix	Macintosh	DOS
text file	.	📄	<F>
directory	/	📁	<D>
phone-book server	<CSO>	📇	<P>
binhexed file	<HQX>	💾	<B>
DOS binary file	<PC Bin>	PC	<B>
uuencoded file	<Bin>	UX	<B>
index search	<?>	?	<?>
telnet session	<TEL>	🖥	<T>
binary file	<Bin>	UX	<B>
TN3270 session	<3270>	🖥	<T>

Figure 1-4. A list of major items available on gopher servers and the symbols representing these items on Unix, Macintosh and DOS-based clients.

individuals or computers, and disseminate similar information in different formats. Some of these features are described in chapter 10 of this book.

Notes

1. For more information about the beginnings of WAIS, read Brewster Kahle, "An information system for corporate users: Wide Area Information Servers" (URL=file://dewey.lib.ncsu.edu/pub/stacks/finding/wais-corporate-paper.text or URL=file://think.com/wais/wais-corporate-paper.text).

2. URL=file://dewey.lib.ncsu.edu/pub/stacks/finding/iubio-wais-8b5-c.tar.Z or URL=file://ftp.bio.indiana.edu/util/wais/iubio-wais-8b5-c.tar.Z

3. URL=file://dewey.lib.ncsu.edu/pub/stacks/finding/freeWAIS-0.1.tar.Z or URL=file://ftp.cnidr.org/pub/NIDR.tools/freeWAIS-0.1.tar.Z

4. Sometimes called USENET News, Usenet is a network of computers used for the purposes of discussing common problems and solutions on issues ranging from horticulture to computers to political science. In many respects, USENET News groups are an alternative to listserv lists. These news groups generate many questions that get asked over and over again. Consequently, the owners of the news groups regularly distribute these questions along with their answers in order to spare the regular users of the news groups the agony of continually reading the same thing. These distributions are called "FAQs."

5. "Pointing" your Gopher client is terminology used to describe where the resulting Gopher query will be sent.

6. A detailed description of the Gopher protocol can be read in Bob Alberti, "The Internet Gopher protocol: A distributed document search and retrieval protocol" (URL=file://dewey.lib.ncsu.edu/pub/stacks/finding/protocol.txt).

7. This feature is enabled with a program called "jughead." Jughead is described in more detail in chapter 10.

2
PCWAIS, a WAIS Client for DOS Computers

There are a number of WAIS clients for DOS (Intel-based) computers. These programs include clients for computers running Windows as well. This chapter describes PCWAIS, a WAIS client for DOS computers.

To run any WAIS or Gopher client on your Intel-based computer, you need a program to "drive" your Ethernet card and, in turn, connect you to the Internet. The unavailability of a standard application for Intel-based computers to "speak Internet" (TCP/IP) has made the development of many Internet-aware applications slow compared to other computer platforms. The closest thing there is to a standard is a collection of programs called Crynwr packet drivers. These programs are freely distributed and exist for just about every Ethernet card available.[1]

An archive of PCWAIS can be found in a number of places across the Internet.[2] It can also be found in the Finding directory. To extract the archive you will need a copy of pkunzip.exe.[3] This too can be found in the Finding directory. Retrieve the archive and unpack it with the command "pkunzip pcdist.zip". A number of new files will be created:

- pcwais.exe — the WAIS client,
- pcwais.cnf — for client configuration,
- pcwais.typ — for recognizing document types,
- wattcp.cfg — for configuring network connections,
- readme — brief instructions, and
- *.src — a number of source files.

Begin by reading the readme file.

Configuring PCWAIS

Next you will have to edit your configuration files, pcwais.cnf and wattcp.cfg. Pcwias.cnf is a file that PCWAIS will read in order to know where your source files will be saved and where to write temporary files. An example follows:

```
localsourcedir c:\pcwais\
commonsourcedir c:\pcwais\
spoolfile c:\pcwais\jnk.out
```

In this particular case, local source files are saved in the directory c:\pcwais\. Other source files (if they exist) are located in the same directory. The second pointer may be directed to a directory on a network that many people use. Last, the spoolfile is defined as c:\pcwais\jnk.out. This is just a temporary file.

wattcp.cfg is a file to let PCWAIS know about your network. Below is an example:

```
my_ip=152.1.24.115
netmask=255.255.0.0
nameserver=152.1.1.22
gateway=152.1.24.65
domainslist="lib.ncsu.edu"
```

Many, if not most, of these values you may not know. When in doubt consult you systems administrator.

Now you are ready to get started. Assuming you have initialized your Ethernet card with the appropriate Crynwr packet drivers, run PCWAIS by entering "pcwais" at the DOS prompt. You should see something like the screen in Figure 2-1.

PCWAIS is capable of being driven by a mouse. If you don't have a mouse, then you can select the functions by pressing the Alt key along with the highlighted letters, or you can use the Tab key to navigate around the screen.

Searching the Directory-of-Servers

A good place to always start, especially if you don't know which databases to search, is to search the directory-of-servers. The

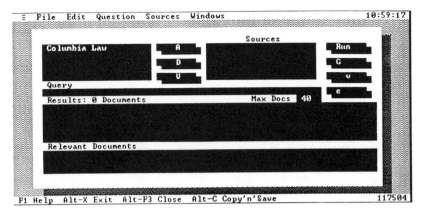

Figure 2-1. The initial display for the PCWAIS WAIS client.

directory-of-servers is a database of databases. Select directory-of-servers from the Available field and add it to the Sources field.

In this particular example, a search was conducted for the term "agriculture" by entering "agriculture" into the Query field and selecting the Run button. The results from this search are displayed in Figure 2-2. When the user selects an item, PCWAIS retrieves the selected document and displays it on the screen as shown in Figure 2-3.

This text describes the source "agricultural-market-news.src." It lists the name and IP number of the computer hosting the information. It lists the version of the WAIS indexer that

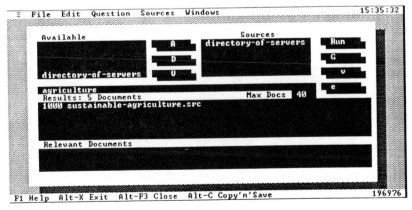

Figure 2-2. The results window of the PCWAIS WAIS client.

```
 ≡  File   Edit   Question   Sources   Windows                  15:47:23
[■]═══════════════════════ Untitled ══════════════════[↕]═
Headline:   291 agricultural-market-news.src
(:source
    :version   3
    :ip-address "128.193.124.4"
    :ip-name "nostromo.oes.orst.edu"
    :tcp-port 210
    :database-name "agricultural-market-news"
    :cost 0.00
    :cost-unit :free
    :maintainer "wais@nostromo.oes.orst.edu"
    :subjects "business  marketing  commodities agriculture agricultural"
    :description "Server created with WAIS release 8 b3.1 on Oct  5 22:48:47 19
1 by wais@nostromo.oes.orst.edu

This server contains the agricultural commodity market reports compiled
by the Agricultural Market News Service of the United States Department
of Agriculture. There are approximately 1200 reports from all over the
United States. Most of these reports are updated daily. Try searching for
'portland grain.'

For more information contact: wais@oes.orst.edu
═══════════════ 1:1 ═══════════════════════════════════════╝
 F1 Help   Alt-X Exit   Alt-F3 Close   Alt-C Copy'n'Save      183760
```

Figure 2-3. The display of a retrieved document from PCWAIS.

created the data. It should also list the name of the person who maintains the database. Last, this source information will also tell you a bit about the information that was indexed. Is it full text? Bibliographic? Graphical?

This source may be one you want to search in the future. Before you save it, you may want to edit the text after the word "Headline:" and before the first "(". The text that appears in this position will be the text displayed in your Available field. To save the source information select the File/Save menu option. When you select this option, the following window will appear (see Figure 2-4).

Figure 2-4. Saving a WAIS source file with PCWAIS.

Enter a name you want to give the source document. As you know, the name can be no longer than eleven characters, and the three characters following the period must be "src" to identify the file as a source document.

Continue searching the directory-of-servers and saving source documents until you feel you have exhausted the possible list of databases to search.

Searching the Rest of WAISspace

Now it is time to search for real information instead of meta-information.

Suppose you were interested in pigs, and you had identified agricultural-market-news and sustainable-agriculture as good sources for this information. You would first put these two sources in your Sources field and enter the term "pigs" into the Query field. Next, run the search by selecting the Run button. Optionally, you can enter an integer in the Max Docs field to limit the number of items PCWAIS retrieves. (See Figure 2-5.)

PCWAIS will then search all the databases listed in your Sources field for your search term(s). Like using the directory-of-servers, you can select located items from the Results field, and PCWAIS will retrieve those items for you and display them.

The screen shown in Figure 2-6 describes the number of pigs and hogs sold on Tuesday, June 8, 1993.

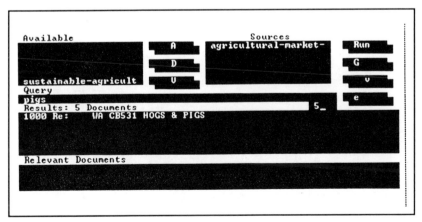

Figure 2-5. Limiting the number of result items with PCWAIS.

```
┌[■]══════════════════════════ Untitled ══════════════════════[‡]═┐
│Headline:  262 Re:    SJ LS250 FEEDER PIGS                        │
│Subject:    SJ LS250 FEEDER PIGS                                  │
│Date: Tue, 08 Jun 93 01:34:20 PM                                  │
│                                                                  │
│SJ LS250                                                          │
│ST. JOSEPH, MO.              TUESDAY - JUNE 8, 1993        USDA    │
│                          FEEDER PIG AUCTION                       │
│RECEIPTS:  2000.                                                   │
│                                                                  │
│    FEEDER PIG PRICES UNEVEN, AVERAGING NEAR STEAD, EXCEPT 60-70 LB PIGS,│
│5.00-8.00 HIGHER.   SEVERAL REPUTATION LONG STRINGS OF ONE OWNER PIG IN THE│
│RUN.   PRICES PER HEAD.   ACTUAL WEIGHTS.                          │
│                                                                  │
│    US 1-2               21 LBS            28.00                   │
│                      32-33 LBS            32.50-34.00             │
│                      36-38 LBS            34.00-41.50             │
│            REPUTATION    38 LBS           45.00                   │
│                      40-50 LBS            40.00-44.00             │
└══════ 1:1 ═══════════════════════════════════════════════════┘
```

Figure 2-6. Another results window in PCWAIS.

Relevance

PCWAIS offers a form a relevance feedback; it provides a solution to the age-old problem of "find me more articles like this one."

To use the relevance feedback mechanism, select a document and click the Relate button. Consequently, your selected document's title will appear in the Relevant Documents field (see Figure 2-7).

Now when you do another search, all the terms from the relevant document will be included in your query.

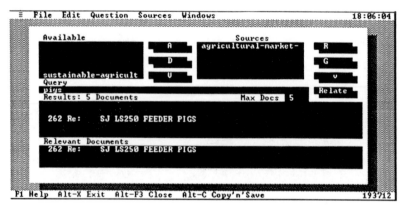

Figure 2-7. Selecting relevant documents with PCWAIS.

Figure 2-8. Creating WAIS source files with PCWAIS.

Creating Your Own Source Information

Not all sources are registered with the directory-of-servers. This does not mean you can't search them. All you have to do is create your own source information.

Suppose you heard about a WAIS index called "ell.src". You heard that it was hosted on dewey.lib.ncsu.edu on port 210. Using the Source/New menu option you are presented with the dialog box in Figure 2-8. You can now enter the appropriate information into the fields and search the database.

After you select the Save button the same Save dialog box will appear that you saw earlier, and you have now added ell.src to your local list of databases (see Figure 2-9).

Figure 2-9. A list of source files in PCWAIS.

Notes

1. URL=file://dewey.lib.ncsu.edu/pub/stacks/finding/driver10.zip or URL=file://boombox.micro.umn.edu/pub/gopher/PC_client/packet-drivers/driver10.zip. You will also need the uncompression program pkunzip.exe to extract your packet driver from the archive (URL=file://dewey.lib.ncsu.edu/pub/stacks/finding/pkunzip.exe).
2. URL=file://dewey.lib.ncsu.edu/pub/stacks/finding/pcdist.zip or URL=file://sunsite.oit.unc.edu/pub/wais/DOS/pcdist.zip
3. URL=file://dewey.lib.ncsu.edu/pub/stacks/finding/pkunzip.exe

3

PC Gopher III, a Gopher Client for DOS Computers

There are several Gopher clients for DOS and Windows (Intel-based) computers. This chapter describes PC Gopher III, a Gopher client distributed by the University of Minnesota.

To use this client your Ethernet card needs to have been initialized with a Crynwr packet driver. This software configures your hardware for "speaking Internet" (TCP/IP).

PC Gopher III can be downloaded from a number of places across the Internet.[1] It is also available in the Finding directory. If you do not have the packet drivers, they are available in the Finding directory.[2]

Download PC Gopher III distribution and uncompress it with the command "pkunzip pcg3.zip". The result will be a number of new files:

- gopher.exe—the PC Gopher III program,
- gopher.bmk—a bookmark file,
- pcg3.doc—documentation in Microsoft Word for Windows,
- pcg3.txt—documentation in text (ASCII) format,
- bmkcvt.exe—bookmark updater,
- bmkcvt.txt—documentation for bmkcvt.exe,
- release.102—release notes PC Gopher III, and
- manifest.102—a list of the files in the archive.

Assuming you have initialized your Ethernet hardware with the proper Crynwr packet driver, run PC Gopher III with the command "gopher". A blank screen should appear.

PC Gopher III is designed to work with a mouse. If you don't have a mouse, then use the Alt key in conjunction with the highlighted letters to open menus and select the buttons.

Configuration

The first thing you will have to do is configure PC Gopher III's application and network setups. Begin with the network configuration by selecting the Configure/Network... menu option, and the window will appear as shown in Figure 3-1.

Many of these items may be unfamiliar to you. Ask your systems administrator for the values for your specific computer.

If your connection is via SLIP (Serial Line IP), then you will want to click the Slip Settings button. Otherwise, if your connection to the Internet is not through a serial line, then you will want to click the Ethernet Settings button. In either case, if you have trouble with timeout errors, then consider editing the numbers displayed to compensate. The default value usually works well.

Click OK to save your network settings.

Next you will have to configure PC Gopher III's application settings. Open the Configure/Application... menu, and you will see the screen shown in Figure 3-2.

Primarily, this is where you tell PC Gopher what Gopher server you want to access first. Enter the Internet name and port number of the Gopher server you want to use by default in the first two fields. Enter a secondary server in the third and fourth fields. When you start a new Gopher, PC Gopher III will randomly pick the first or second server you specify. Unless the server you will be trying to connect to is not duplicated on another computer with a different address, then enter the same name in

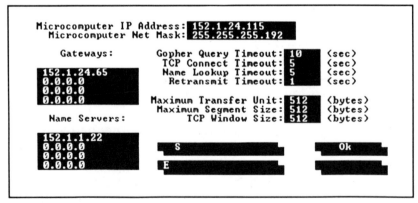

Figure 3-1. Configuring PC Gopher's network options.

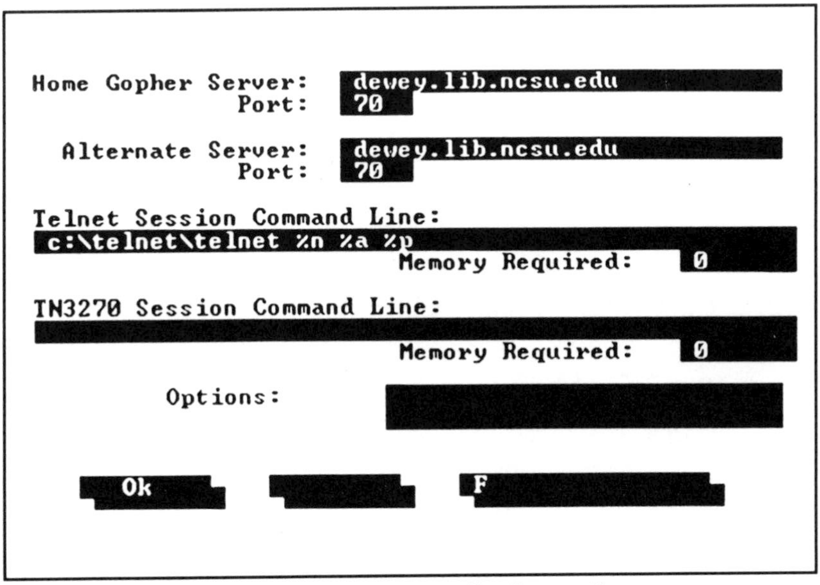

```
Home Gopher Server:   dewey.lib.ncsu.edu
              Port:   70

   Alternate Server:   dewey.lib.ncsu.edu
              Port:   70

Telnet Session Command Line:
   c:\telnet\telnet %n %a %p
                   Memory Required:     0

TN3270 Session Command Line:

                   Memory Required:     0

        Options:


        Ok              F
```

Figure 3-2. Configuring PC Gopher's application options.

the first and third fields, or don't enter any information in the third and fourth fields.

In order for PC Gopher to run a remote login session, you must specify the command to run your terminal program. Enter the full path name of your telnet program in the fifth field. Then enter "%a", "%n", and "%p" as well. These are placeholders for Internet address, Internet name, and port. Don't worry about the Memory Required field unless you seem to be having problems telneting. In this case, enter an integer here specifying the amount of RAM your telnet program requires. The same procedure holds true for the tn3270 files.

Check the New Gopher on Startup button if you want PC Gopher III to automatically open a connection to your specified server when you run PC Gopher. Check Single Window Mode if you want to see only the current window while navigating Gopherspace. (Personally, I like this option because it keeps my screen less cluttered.)

Finally, click the OK button, and your settings will be saved.

Using PC Gopher

Now that you have configured PC Gopher you are ready to go. Select the File/New Gopher menu option and PC Gopher should display the root menu of the server you specified. Using dewey.lib.ncsu.edu on port 70 as an example, the screen should look something like Figure 3-3.

Items in Gopherspace are identified with different letters prefixing each menu. Here is a list of standard items and their meaning:

Symbol	Item
<F>	text file
<D>	directory
<?>	index search
<T>	telnet or tn3270 remote login session
<B>	PC binary file
<B>	Macintosh BinHex file
<B>	Unix uuencoded file
<P>	CSO phonebook

Each one of these items will be described in turn.

Items marked with an <F> are text files. By double-clicking on a menu item (or using the arrow keys and pressing Enter), the files associated with the menu item will be displayed. By

Figure 3-3. The main menu of the gopher at the NCSU Libraries as viewed with PC Gopher.

selecting the <F> from the menu above, the window shown in Figure 3-4 will appear.

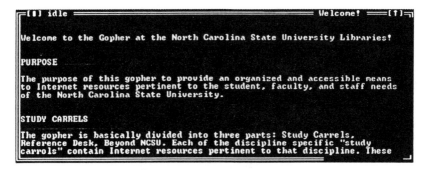

Figure 3-4. A text file as displayed with PC Gopher.

You can now scroll up and down this text. You can also save it by using the File/Save File... menu option.

Items marked with a <D> are directories. By selecting these items, more menu choices appear. Once you select a directory, to go back to the previous directory, click (or select) the Go Back button.

Index searches are marked with the <?> symbol. These items may be WAIS indexes, or they may be some other type of index. The thing all index searches have in common is the ability to take a query from the user and apply that query to a database. In the opening screen of the Gopher at the NCSU Libraries there is an item named "Search this gopher." This particular index search is a jughead search, and it will produce a list of menu items within the server matching your query. (jughead is described in more detail in chapter 10.)

When you select an index search item the dialog box in Figure 3-5 appears.

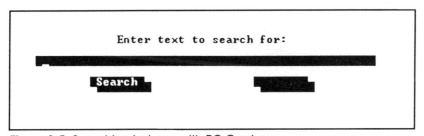

Figure 3-5. Searching indexes with PC Gopher.

The form of your query depends on the type of index the menu item represents. In this case, a jughead search, your query can take a single argument, a simple string, for example "library." The server will then search its index for menu items containing the term "library." This search results in the menu as shown in Figure 3-6.

From here the user can select any of these items and use them just as if the user had found them by navigating the menu.

WAIS searches in PC Gopher work the same way. For example, if you select "NCSU's 'Library Without Walls'"/Stacks/ALCTS, then you will be in a directory containing the entire collection of the ALCTS Network News. The menu item Search ALCTS Network News is a pointer to a WAIS index. By selecting this item you can query the index and locate information from the entire collection of ALCTS Network News. The screen shown in Figure 3-7 is the output from a search for "NREN" ("National Research and Education Network").

Thus, PC Gopher performed as a WAIS client to an index of electronic serials. By selecting any of the listed items you can read and save them.

Your PC Gopher client can also initiate telnet or tn3270 remote login sessions for you. This will depend upon whether you have a telnet or tn3270 program on your computer, as well as whether you configured PC Gopher correctly under the Configure/Application... menu item.

Items marked with a <T> are remote login sessions. In the opening menu of the Gopher at the NCSU Libraries is a listing

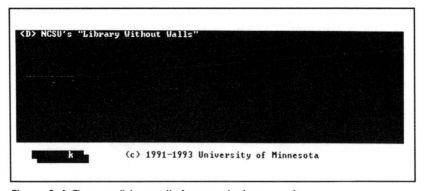

Figure 3-6. The possible results from an index search.

Figure 3-7. Search results of a WAIS index using PC Gopher.

for North Carolina State University's campus-wide information system, Happenings! If you select Happenings!, you will be reminded of the password to log on to the remote service. (See Figure 3-8.)

Click OK, and if everything is configured correctly, your terminal application will run and open up a connection to the service automatically. Figure 3-9 shows what your screen may look like.

After you log off from the remote service you will be put back into PC Gopher to continue your expeditions through Gopherspace.

Items marked <B> are binary files. Binary files are usually computer programs, but they may also be compressed text files. The binary files may be in a Macintosh format, a Unix format, or a DOS format. It is hoped the server you are connected to will give you some indication of what type of platform the binary file is intended for.

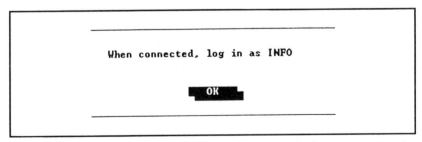

Figure 3-8. PC Gopher reminds you of passwords for connecting to remote login services.

```
         North Carolina State University Computing Center VAX 8700

*************************************************************************
*           Happenings!, your campuswide information system, and       *
*                     PUBLIC Software Access Facility                   *
*                                                                      *
*        Access to Happenings! is available by typing INFO at the      *
*        USERNAME: prompt following this message.                      *
*                                                                      *
*        PUBLIC may be accessed by entering PUBLIC at the USERNAME:     *
*        prompt.  If you have any problems, please contact a consultant *
*        at (919) 515-3035.                                            *
*                                                                      *
*        Please make sure you are emulating a DEC VT100, 200 or 300    *
*        style terminal; VT100 is the default.                         *
*************************************************************************
PUBLIC Users:   We are having difficulty with FTP file transfer.  This will
                be corrected ASAP.  Please accept our apologies for any
                inconvenience this may cause.

Username: INFO
  ccvax1.cc.ncsu                                                    18 17
```

Figure 3-9. A possible display once connected to a remote login service.

Navigate the Gopher at the NCSU Libraries to NCSU's "Library Without Walls"/Software tool for gathering information/DOS tools and you should see a few programs listed there. By selecting any of these items you have the opportunity to download those files. In Figure 3-10, PCWAIS client 1.03 was selected, and you are presented with a dialog box prompting you for a file name specification.

One of greatest things about Gopher is its ability to save these sorts of files. Since many Gopher servers point to ftp sites, you can use your Gopher client to navigate these ftp sites and

```
  C:\GOPHER\PCDIST.ZIP                          OK

  iles
  3C507.COM

```

Figure 3-10. A PC Gopher prompt for saving a binary file.

download files. This can all be done without knowing a single ftp command!

Be forewarned. Do not download Macintosh or Unix binary files unless you are going to upload them to a Macintosh or Unix computer. Your DOS machine will not be able to read these files.

Last, items marked with a <P> are CSO phonebooks. These are databases of names, addresses, telephone numbers, and miscellaneous information. These databases usually apply to universities. When selecting a <P> you will be presented with a dialog box much like the typical <?> items (see Figure 3-11).

Figure 3-11. Searching CSO phone books with PC Gopher.

Here you can enter any text you want. Alternatively, you can click the More Choices... button to create a more sophisticated search (see Figure 3-12).

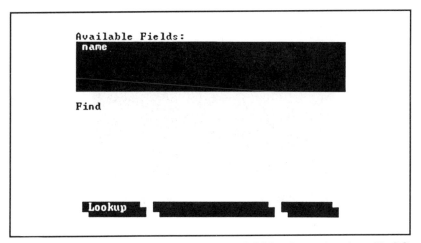

Figure 3-12. More complex searching of CSO phone books with PC Gopher.

By using the arrow key and pressing Return you are given the opportunity to search that field. Return to the Available Fields field to select other fields to search. Each term in the selected fields will be combined with a Boolean "and."

Bookmarks

As you cruise Gopherspace you may discover menu items that you wish to access over and over again. Accessing them can get tedious, especially if a particular item is at the bottom of some remote menu. This is why bookmarks were invented.

Bookmarks are placeholders in Gopherspace. When you locate an item you particularly like, and you believe you will use this item frequently, then select Open Bookmark List from the File menu. A new dialog box will appear. By clicking the Add button you will be prompted for a name to be given to your currently selected menu item. After you enter that name, the menu item will be added to your list of bookmarks. (See Figure 3-13.)

Now whenever you want to access that particular menu item, all you have to do is select Open Bookmark List from the File menu and then select an item from your bookmarks. PC Gopher will then retrieve that item for you.

Keep in mind that the Internet, and therefore Gopher, is in a constant state of flux. One day you may be able to access your marked item, but the next day you may not. This may happen

Figure 3-13. Bookmarks in PC Gopher.

because the server at the other end of the line is down or the service may have changed its IP number. Another possibility is that the server's administrator has reorganized the server's menu structure and therefore your bookmark points to an invalid location.

Notes

1. Try URL=file://boombox.micro.umn.edu/pub/gopher/PC_client/pcg3.zip or URL=file://dewey.lib.ncsu.edu/pub/stacks/finding/pcg3.zip. You will also need the uncompression program, pkunzip.exe, URL=file://dewey.lib.ncsu.edu/pub/stacks/finding/pkunzip.exe.
2. URL=file://dewey.lib.ncsu.edu/pub/stacks/finding/driver10.zip or URL=file://boombox.micro.umn.edu/pub/gopher/PC_client/packet-drivers/driver10.zip. You will also need the uncompression program pkunzip.exe to extract your packet driver from the archive (URL=file://dewey.lib.ncsu.edu/pub/stacks/finding/pkunzip.exe).

4

Simple WAIS, a Unix Curses Client for WAIS

This chapter describes the Simple WAIS client commonly referred to as SWAIS.

As the embedded history text of the SWAIS client says, "It [SWAIS] provides most of the functionality of the more complicated interfaces but features a simple and potentially more natural interface." (Some people would disagree with the last half of this statement.)

Getting Started and Moving Around

SWAIS is a WAIS client for Unix computers running in vt100 terminal mode. Typically, SWAIS is launched via a shell script (swais.sh) that sets the environment variable WAISCOMMON-SOURCEDIR, a pointer to the directory containing your WAIS .src files. The shell script then launches the SWAIS program, resulting in a screen like Figure 4-1.

```
▤☐▤▤▤▤▤▤▤▤▤▤▤▤▤ UT100 terminal window ▤▤▤▤▤▤▤▤▤▤▤▤▤☐▤
SWAIS                          Source Selection              Sources: 283 ⇧
  #          Server                      Source                      Cost
001:  [         archie.au]  aarnet-resource-guide                    Free
002:  [weeds.mgh.harvard.ed]  AAtDB                                  Free
003:  [    archive.orst.edu]  aeronautics                            Free
004:  [ bloat.media.mit.edu]  Aesop-Fables                           Free
005:  [nostromo.oes.orst.ed]  agricultural-market-news               Free
006:  [    archive.orst.edu]  alt.drugs                              Free
007:  [    wais.oit.unc.edu]  alt.gopher                             Free
008:  [sun-wais.oit.unc.edu]  alt.sys.sun                            Free
009:  [    wais.oit.unc.edu]  alt.wais                               Free
010:  [        150.203.76.2]  ANU-Aboriginal-Studies         $0.00/minute
011:  [   coombs.anu.edu.au]  ANU-Asian-Religions            $0.00/minute
012:  [        150.203.76.2]  ANU-Pacific-Linguistics        $0.00/minute
013:  [   coombs.anu.edu.au]  ANU-Pacific-Manuscripts                Free
014:  [   coombs.anu.edu.au]  ANU-SocSci-Netlore             $0.00/minute
015:  [        150.203.76.2]  ANU-SSDA-Catalogues            $0.00/minute
016:  [   coombs.anu.edu.au]  ANU-Thai-Yunnan                        Free
017:  [    quake.think.com]  Applications-Navigator                  Free
018:  [      132.183.190.21]  Arabidopsis-BioSci                     Free

Keywords:

<space> selects, w for keywords, arrows move, <return> searches, q quits, or ? ⇩
◁▯                                                                        ▷▯
```

Figure 4-1. A sample display from the SWAIS WAIS client.

31

This screen lists the first eighteen sources saved in your sources directory. The integer in the upper right-hand corner represents the number of sources you have to choose from. The second item on the second line lists the Internet name of the computer (server) hosting the index (source) listed in the third column. The fourth column lists the cost of the database. (The costs feature of WAIS is not implemented yet. Presently all sources are free.)

Simple online help is provided by pressing "h." To quit SWAIS press "q." To move up and down the list of sources, use the arrow keys on your keyboard, or press "j" or "k." To move to a particular source, enter its number or enter a slash (/) followed by some text.

Using WAIS

Suppose you wanted to find information about astronomy. If you don't know which source(s) to search, the best place to start is the directory-of-servers. The directory-of-servers is an index of WAIS indexes. As new WAIS indexes are created, maintainers of the indexes are encouraged to register their work, complete with text describing the index and its contents. This registration will then become part of the directory-of-servers. When you search the directory-of-servers, you are searching the text describing the indexes.

To search the directory-of-servers, navigate to the directory-of-servers listing using the arrow keys. By pressing the space bar you select a source for searching. Selected indexes are marked with an asterisk (see Figure 4-2).

To view the description of a source, press "v." The resulting text is the text sent to the directory-of-servers describing the source. It contains computer information as well as descriptive information (see Figure 4-3).

Whenever you see "—More—" at the bottom of the screen you can press the space bar to continue paging through the text. Alternatively, you can press "q" to stop viewing the text.

When you stop viewing the descriptive text and the list of sources is displayed, press "w" for "words." Enter your search terms. After entering your term(s), press the Enter or Return

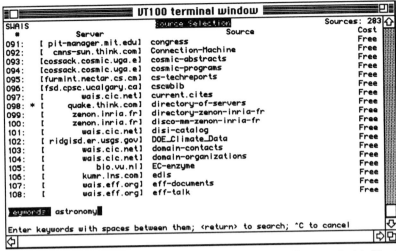

Figure 4-2. Selected sources in SWAIS are marked with an asterisk (*).

key. SWAIS will now formulate a query, send it off to the directory-of-servers, wait, and display the results. Figure 4-4 shows the results from a query on the word "astronomy."

In this case, there were six servers found that were described with the term "astronomy." The second column of the

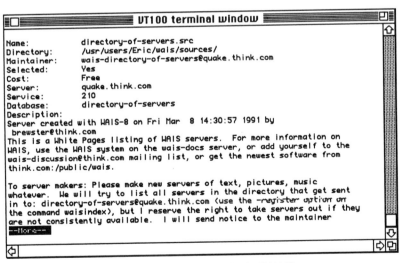

Figure 4-3. The display of a WAIS source file in SWAIS.

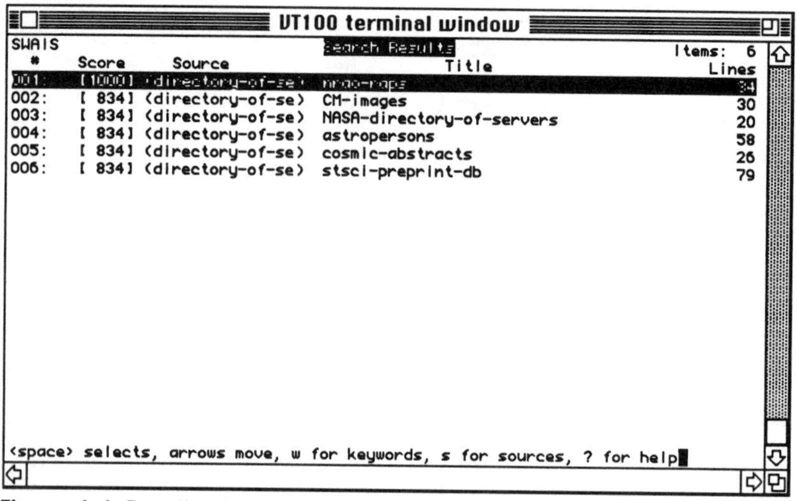

Figure 4-4. Results of a search of the directory-of-servers using the term "astronomy".

second line lists the located document's score. Depending on the WAIS indexer used to create the source, a document's score may very well be based on the number of times your search term(s) was found in the document, the position of the term in the document, and the length of the document.[1] The third column lists the source you searched. The fourth column lists the title of the document.

To retrieve any of the documents, use the arrow keys to highlight the desired document and then press the space bar. SWAIS will again formulate a new query, send it to the server, wait, and display the results. Figure 4-5 shows the results from selecting item 1, nroa-raps.

An undocumented retrieval feature of SWAIS is the "m" command. By using "m" you can mail the results of a search to yourself or anybody else. Simply select a title, press "m," and enter the recipient's e-mail address.

Once you have searched the directory-of-servers and identified the sources of interest, take note of the sources' names and use "s" to return to the main screen listing the WAIS source (database) files.

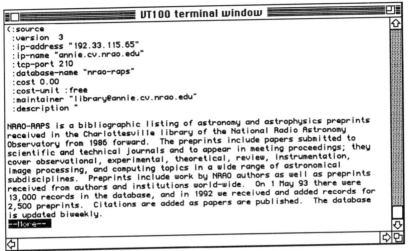

```
▓□▓▓▓▓▓▓▓▓▓▓▓▓▓▓▓▓▓ UT100 terminal window ▓▓▓▓▓▓▓▓▓▓▓▓▓□▓
( :source                                                    ⇧
 :version  3
 :ip-address "192.33.115.65"
 :ip-name "annie.cv.nrao.edu"
 :tcp-port 210
 :database-name "nrao-raps"
 :cost 0.00
 :cost-unit :free
 :maintainer "library@annie.cv.nrao.edu"
 :description "

NRAO-RAPS is a bibliographic listing of astronomy and astrophysics preprints
received in the Charlottesville library of the National Radio Astronomy
Observatory from 1986 forward.  The preprints include papers submitted to
scientific and technical journals and to appear in meeting proceedings; they
cover observational, experimental, theoretical, review, instrumentation,
image processing, and computing topics in a wide range of astronomical
subdisciplines.  Preprints include work by NRAO authors as well as preprints
received from authors and institutions world-wide.  On 1 May 93 there were
13,000 records in the database, and in 1992 we received and added records for
2,500 preprints.  Citations are added as papers are published.  The database
is updated biweekly.
--More--                                                     ⇩
◁                                                          ▷▣
```

Figure 4-5. The display of another source file in SWAIS.

Searching the Rest of WAISspace

One of the unique features of WAIS clients is their ability to search more than one database at a time. Use "s" to navigate the list of sources and use the space bar to select databases you want to search. Keep in mind the items you located from the directory-of-servers.

In this particular example, a new search is attempted on all the indexes "recommended" by the directory-of-servers and illustrated in Figure 4-4. Using the "/" command allows you to enter a WAIS database name and locate it quickly. Thus all the sources were located but one. This points out a difficulty with WAIS and the Internet in general. These things are dynamic. One day a service may exist, and another day it is gone. One day a service may be located on one computer, and the next day the same service has moved to another computer. All this happens because there is no central authority governing the use of the Internet. As you "surf" the Internet you will come to appreciate, tolerate, and be annoyed by the Internet's dynamic features.

After your sources are selected, press "w" to enter your search terms. In this case, a search was done for "black holes." This search produced the screen in Figure 4-6.

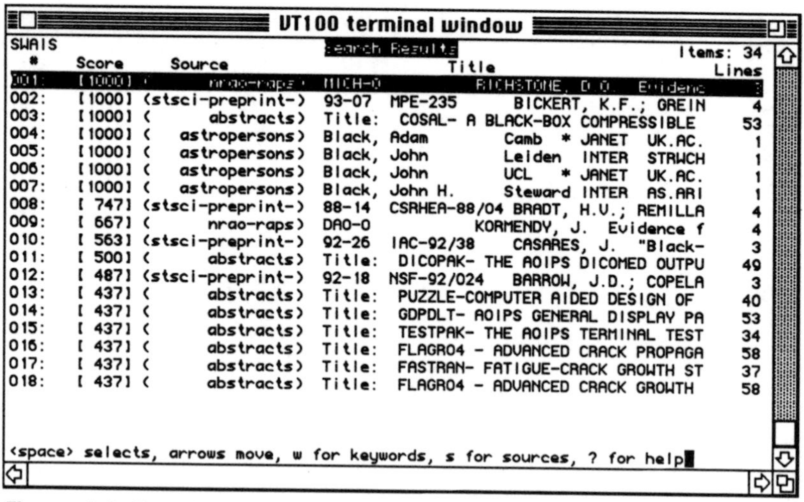

```
≣□▨▬▬▬▬▬▬▬▬▬▬ UT100 terminal window ▬▬▬▬▬▬▬▬▬▬█回▨
SWAIS                        Search Results                    Items: 34  ⇧
 #      Score      Source                  Title                         Lines
001:   [1000]    nrao-raps     MICH-O        RICHSTONE, D. O. Evidenc      2
002:   [1000] (stsci-preprint-) 93-07 MPE-235    BICKERT, K.F.; GREIN      4
003:   [1000] (     abstracts) Title:  COSAL- A BLACK-BOX COMPRESSIBLE     53
004:   [1000] (  astropersons) Black, Adam       Camb  * JANET  UK.AC.     1
005:   [1000] (  astropersons) Black, John       Leiden  INTER  STRWCH     1
006:   [1000] (  astropersons) Black, John       UCL   * JANET  UK.AC.     1
007:   [1000] (  astropersons) Black, John H.     Steward INTER  AS.ARI    1
008:   [ 747] (stsci-preprint-) 88-14 CSRHEA-88/04 BRADT, H.V.; REMILLA     4
009:   [ 667] (     nrao-raps) DAO-O            KORMENDY, J. Evidence f    4
010:   [ 563] (stsci-preprint-) 92-26 IAC-92/38    CASARES, J.  "Black-     3
011:   [ 500] (     abstracts) Title:  DICOPAK- THE AOIPS DICOMED OUTPU    49
012:   [ 487] (stsci-preprint-) 92-18 NSF-92/024   BARROW, J.D.; COPELA     3
013:   [ 437] (     abstracts) Title:  PUZZLE-COMPUTER AIDED DESIGN OF     40
014:   [ 437] (     abstracts) Title:  GDPDLT- AOIPS GENERAL DISPLAY PA    53
015:   [ 437] (     abstracts) Title:  TESTPAK- THE AOIPS TERMINAL TEST    34
016:   [ 437] (     abstracts) Title:  FLAGRO4 - ADVANCED CRACK PROPAGA    58
017:   [ 437] (     abstracts) Title:  FASTRAN- FATIGUE-CRACK GROWTH ST    37
018:   [ 437] (     abstracts) Title:  FLAGRO4 - ADVANCED CRACK GROWTH     58



<space> selects, arrows move, w for keywords, s for sources, ? for help▮    ⇩
◁                                                                    ▷◱
```

Figure 4-6. The display of a search for "black holes" from sources containing the term "astronomy".

Notice the last column. It shows you the number of lines in the document you located.

By using the arrow keys and selecting documents with the space bar, the documents are retrieved from the server. In this case, the retrieved list did contain a few citations. Most of them were written by people named "Black." There were a couple of descriptions of astronomical programs. Ironically, the item at the very bottom of the list with the lowest score was a relevant citation on black holes.

WAIS is capable of indexing files other than text files. For example, it can index graphic files of the Tagged Image File Format (TIFF) or the Macintosh picture (PICT) format. SWAIS, on the other hand, cannot display these files. So if you search a source with SWAIS that contains images, then you will not be able to retrieve the images.

Summary

SWAIS is a useful client, but not one of the friendliest ones. Like the other WAIS clients, its purpose is to first search indexes of data and then retrieve documents from the server. It has all the features of the Macintosh and DOS clients except the relevance feedback option. This is a major deficiency. Nor does it have the ability to save located documents to disk, but the mail feature can, in some ways, compensate for this.

Incidentally, with the Thinking Machines distribution of WAIS there is a program called waissearch. It is a command-line WAIS client. It too runs in vt100 terminal mode. Since it runs from the command line, it has a number of possibilities for inclusion in shell scripts. One such example will be described as Alcuin in chapter 10.

Note

1. Reread chapter 1 for a more detailed description of WAIS's relevance-weighting algorithms.

5
Gopher, a Unix Curses Client

This chapter describes how to use the Unix Gopher curses client version 2.08.[1] Curses is a method of displaying stylized text on a vt100 screen.

The Unix curses client is invoked with the command "gopher". It requires, at a minimum, a vt100 terminal. The command has the following form:

```
gopher [-sb] [-t title] [-p path] [hostname port]
```

where all the parameters are optional. -S specifies "secure mode," which means that you won't be able to save or print the files that you browse. -B starts the client on the bookmark page. (Bookmarks will be described later in this chapter.) -T specifies the title the root screen will display. -P designates an optional selector string you may use to go anywhere in Gopherspace.[2] Hostname designates the name of the computer where a Gopher server resides. Think of the port as a telephone extension. Most Gopher servers are located on port 70.

The reason all these parameters are optional is that the Gopher program has been compiled (built) with default values for these options.

To make your life simple, just enter "gopher". The Gopher client on dewey.lib.ncsu.edu has been set up to point to dewey.lib.ncsu.edu on port 70. When the client is run, the screen shown in Figure 5-1 is what is initially displayed.

You can navigate Gopherspace in three ways: with arrow keys, menu number selection, and letters. For example, use the arrow keys on your keyboard to move up and down the menus, and press Return. Optionally, press the number of the menu item and press Return. To go back one menu (the previous menu), press "u." To go to the root (first) menu press "m."

Figure 5-1. The gopher curses client display of the main menu of the Gopher at the NCSU Libraries.

To quit the curses client enter "q" or "Q". "Q" quits immediately and "q" allows you to confirm the procedure. A simple help file is available by entering "?".

Using the "/" key is another way to navigate Gopher menus with the curses client. By typing a "/" you are prompted for a term. Enter the term, and the case-sensitive string will be located in the menu, if it exists. Use the "/" again and the next occurrence of the term will be found. Note that the term will be located in any part of any word in the menu. Consequently, if you enter a "t", then you will find all the menu items containing a "t." Be specific.

As you "surf" Gopherspace with the curses client, menu items will be terminated with symbols representing the type of Gopher item it is. Here is a list of the standard symbols:

Type	Symbol
text file	.
directory	/
phonebook server	<CSO>
binhexed file	<HQX>
DOS binary file	<PC Bin>
uuencoded file	<Bin>
index search	<?>

Type	Symbol
telnet session	<TEL>
binary file	<Bin>
tn3270 session	<3270>
ASK block	<??>

Text files are ASCII files. Directories are containers of more menu items. Phonebook servers are databases of names, addresses, telephone numbers, and notes about people. Binhexed files are ASCII versions of Macintosh binary files. DOS binary files are just that, files that run on DOS machines. Index searches are items that allow you to search server-defined databases (many times WAIS indexes). Binary files are binary files for Unix computers. Telnet and tn3270 sessions are connections to remote computers via the telnet (a communications) protocol. Finally, ASK blocks are forms completed by the user and then processed by the server.

Each of these items will be examined below.

Selecting the first item (About the Gopher at the NCSU Libraries) from the server on dewey.lib.ncsu.edu results in the screen shown in Figure 5-2.

All text files, like the help file, are displayed via a pager program. This is sometimes the Unix "more" program, but depending on how your client was built, it may be the pager program

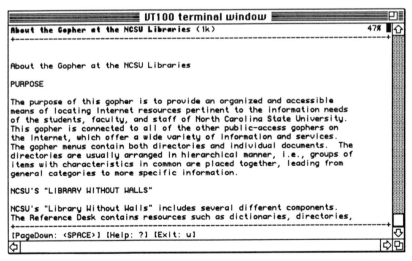

Figure 5-2. The display of a text file using the gopher curses client.

developed by the University of Minnesota. If the text file you are browsing is longer than one screen, then press the space bar and another screen of text will be displayed. (Use the Unix manual to learn more about "more" or enter a "?" to get help about the University of Minnesota pager.)

When you are finished browsing a text file you may have the option of mailing it to an e-mail address.[3] Enter "m" before returning to the menu, and you will be prompted for an e-mail address. Enter an e-mail address and press Return. The text will be delivered. Be forewarned. Do not send very large text files, because they may crash the e-mail program of the Unix computer or of the computer of the recipient.

If the client was not invoked with the -s option, then you will also be given the opportunity to save or print the text file. You can use these options when pointing to a text item as well as at the end of the browsing process. The ability to perform these options depends on your Unix computer's configuration.

All index searches, items terminated by <?>, work similarly, except that the format of the search strategies may be slightly different. Returning back to the main menu and selecting item 4, "Search this gopher (jughead)" results in an index search and the screen shown in Figure 5-3.

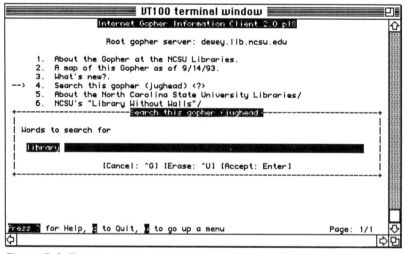

Figure 5-3. The prompt for searching an index using the gopher curses client.

This particular index search is a jughead search, a mini-veronica if you will. (jughead is described in chapter 10. Veronica is discussed in chapter 8.) This screen is prompting you for search terms. The Gopher server will then use your search terms to find data in the database associated with the index represented by the menu item. In this case, search terms are used to locate items in the local Gopher server. For example, a search for "library" returns the screen shown in Figure 5-4.

From here you can select any item from the menu and use that item. Note the bottom right-hand corner where it lists "Page:1/4." This means there is more than one screen of menu items. To get to page 2, 3, or 4, repeatedly press the down arrow keys and the balance of the pages will be displayed. To return to the first page, press the up arrow keys and the process will be reversed.

Index searches of WAIS indexes work the same way. In the Gopher at the NCSU Libraries there is a WAIS index of the complete collection of the electronic serial ALAWON. By navigating to ALAWON and searching it for the term "NREN" the following results are returned (see Figure 5-5).

The results are listed and ranked just as if a WAIS search had been done with the SWAIS client. There are a number of differences. First, you can retrieve no more than forty items in

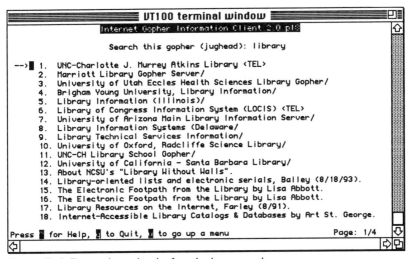

Figure 5-4. Example output of an index search.

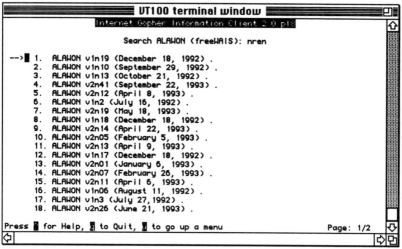

Figure 5-5. The results of a WAIS index search using the gopher curses client.

any one search.[4] Second, there is no way to search multiple indexes with one query. Again, to view the retrieval, all you have to do is select a menu item (see Figure 5-6).

Like any other text file, you can now print, save, or mail the results.

When selecting a <TEL> or <tn3270> item from a Gopher menu (a telnet or tn3270 session), the Gopher curses client will

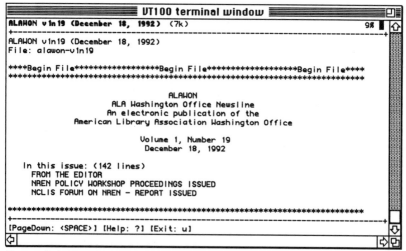

Figure 5-6. Viewing an item from a WAIS index search.

display one or two items of important information. It will always display the address of the remote computer, and if a log-on is required, then it will display a password. Figure 5-7 shows what the screen looks like when you select "NCSU Libraries Information System" from within the "Library Without Walls."

This screen reminds you what you are about to do and what to do if you have any trouble. If the remote service requires a password, then the most important thing this screen does is remind you of the password you may need to log on to the remote service. After making the connection and entering "LIBRARY", Figure 5-8 shows what you see.

When you quit the remote session you are brought back to the Gopher client where you left it.

When you select menu items representing operating system specific files designated by the symbols <PC Bin>, <HQX>, and <Bin> you are prompted for a file name by the curses client as shown in Figure 5-9.

By default, the filename is the same as the menu item. When downloading any file like this, make sure your particular computer can use that file. A Macintosh file will not run on a DOS computer. Nor will a DOS file run on a Unix computer. So if you have only a Unix computer at your disposal, then you should download only Unix files unless you are later going to copy the files to another platform.

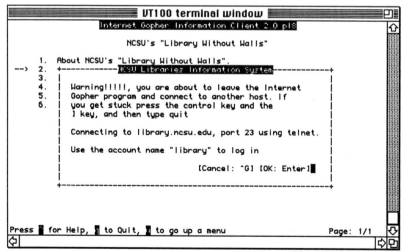

Figure 5-7. The gopher curses client reminds you of user names before connecting you to remote login sessions.

```
═════════════════ UT100 terminal window ════════════════
                          NCSU Libraries

User: LIBRARY                                  Date:  10/08/93
                                               Time:  10:19 AM
NCSU Libraries Information System Main Menu

    A  About the NCSU Libraries Information System

    1  Library Catalogs
    2  Journal Article Indexes
    3  Electronic Journals and Books
    4  Resources On the NCSU Campus
    5  Resources Beyond the NCSU Campus

    L  Log off




Select Option: █
```

Figure 5-8. A possible delay once connected to a remote login session.

Bookmarks

As you navigate Gopherspace you will notice that you use particular menu items frequently. To navigate to these items quickly
you can create bookmarks. Bookmarks are personalized pointers
to remote items in Gopherspace. To create a bookmark with the

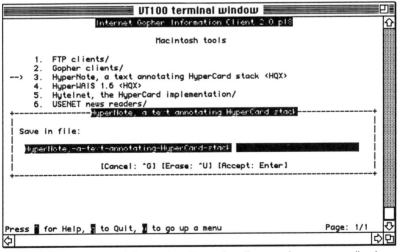

```
═════════════════ UT100 terminal window ════════════════
              Internet Gopher Information Client 2.0 pl8
                          Macintosh tools

        1.  FTP clients/
        2.  Gopher clients/
 -->    3.  HyperNote, a text annotating HyperCard stack <HQX>
        4.  HyperWAIS 1.6 <HQX>
        5.  Hytelnet, the HyperCard implementation/
        6.  USENET news readers/
    +--------------HyperNote, a text annotating HyperCard stack-------------+
    |                                                                       |
    | Save in file:                                                         |
    |                                                                       |
    | HyperNote,-a-text-annotating-HyperCard-stack                          |
    |                                                                       |
    |             [Cancel: ^G] [Erase: ^U] [Accept: Enter]                  |
    +-----------------------------------------------------------------------+




Press █ for Help, █ to Quit, █ to go up a menu          Page: 1/1
```

Figure 5-9. The prompt for saving files using the gopher curses client.

Unix curses client, use the up and down arrow keys to move to the item and then press "a." You will then be prompted for a name for the bookmark (see Figure 5-10).

You can create many bookmarks representing items throughout Gopherspace.

Once you are in a directory, if you find many useful items there you can also save the entire directory with a bookmark. To do this, press "a" and give the item a name.

To view the bookmarks, press "v" and they will be listed. Now you can move through your bookmark list and select those items as if they were any other items.

To remove bookmarks from your bookmark list, first display the bookmarks, select an item from the list, and press "d." This will delete the item from your bookmark list.

ASK Blocks

New features of the Gopher+ protocol include ASK blocks. ASK blocks allow Gopher server administrators to create electronic forms. These forms are then completed by users and processed by the server. ASK blocks are identified in the Unix curses client with double question marks, <??>.

For example, there is a directory in the Gopher at the NCSU Libraries at the root menu called "Suggestion Box and

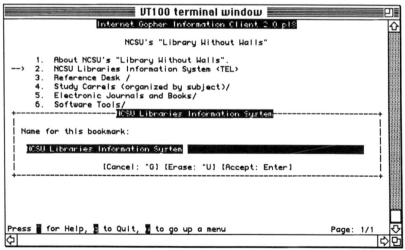

Figure 5-10. Creating bookmarks with the gopher curses client.

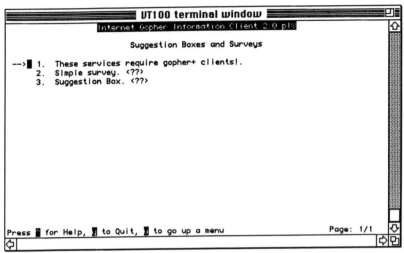

Figure 5-11. ASK blocks as displayed in the menus of a gopher curses client.

Surveys." This directory contains two ASK block items (see Figure 5-11).

When you select item 2, the screen in Figure 5-12 appears.

By following the instructions at the bottom of the screen, you can now complete the form. In this particular case, this form queries the user about his or her location, computer, use

```
═══════════════ UT100 terminal window ═══════════════
+-----------------------Simple survey------------------------+
|                                                            |
| Please take a minute to answer                             |
| a few questions about your use                             |
| of the Gopher at the NCSU Libraries.                       |
| Where are you located?                                     |
| Location                            Off campus█            |
| What is the operating system of your                       |
| primary gopher client?                                     |
| Operating System                    Macintosh             |
| Which section of the Gopher at the                         |
| NCSU Libraries do you use the most?                        |
| Section                             'On campus             |
| How would you classify yourself?                           |
| Classification                      Undergraduate          |
| What is your name? (optional)                              |
| What is your email address? (optional)                     |
| If you have anything to add,                               |
| then please feel free to do it here.                       |
| then please feel free to do it here.                       |
|                                                            |
|      [Switch Fields: TAB] [Cancel: ^G] [Erase: ^U] [Accept: Enter]
|                        [Cycle Values: SPACE]               |
+------------------------------------------------------------+
```

Figure 5-12. ASK blocks as displayed in the gopher curses client.

of the server, university classification, and any additional comments the user would like to make. (It is obvious from the screen that no one could write a very long comment even if desired.)

What happens to these forms once they are completed is entirely up to the server administrator. To learn more about ASK blocks, consult chapter 10.

Notes

1. Curses is a screen-handling package that comes with the Unix operating system. As my man pages say, "These routines give the user a method of updating screens with reasonable optimization. They keep an image of the current screen, and the user sets up an image of a new one."
2. Selector strings are text strings describing a particular item in Gopherspace. Since they are a bit convoluted for a user to enter, they are not described here. Consider reading Bob Alberti, "The Internet Gopher protocol: A distributed document search and retrieval protocol" (URL=file://dewey.lib.ncsu.edu/pub/stacks/finding/protocol.txt) for a complete description.
3. Again, the ability to mail yourself documents from within the Gopher curses client depends on whether or not this feature was built into your client when the client was compiled.
4. This is the default, but it can be changed when the Gopher server is compiled.

6

WAIStation, a WAIS Client for the Macintosh

This chapter describes WAIStation, a WAIS client for the Macintosh. WAIStation was introduced in early 1991 and was written by the folks at Apple when they were working in collaboration with Thinking Machines. There are at least two other WAIS clients for the Macintosh. One is called WAIS for Mac.[1] It, like WAIStation is, free. The other is a HyperCard implementation called HyperWAIS.[2] All three of these clients can be found in the Finding folder.

Just like any other Internet-related software for the Macintosh, WAIStation requires that MacTCP be installed before it will work.

When you initially launch WAIStation, two windows appear: Sources and Questions (see Figures 6-1 and 6-2).

In the Sources window you will save information about the sources (indexes) you search. The Questions window is where you can save the queries you apply to the sources.

Figure 6-1. The initial Sources window of WAIStation.

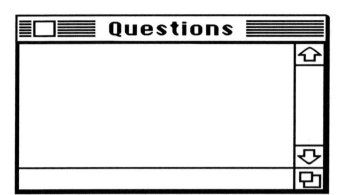

Figure 6-2. The initial Questions window of WAIStation.

Begin by selecting Open Source... from the Source menu. The original distribution of WAIStation includes a Sources folder. Open the Sources folder and select directory-of-servers. A window will appear describing the directory-of-servers (see Figure 6-3).

The most important section of this dialog box is the scrolling field in the center. This field displays a description of the index and its capabilities. This description was written by the information provider. It is hoped it will tell you whether or not this particular index supports Boolean searching, what types of data are included in the database (text, pictures, formatted documents), and when and how often the database is updated. The other fields in this dialog instruct WAIStation regarding the display font, how you are going to connect to the remote database (via TCP, locally, or serially), and how often you are going to search the database.

By clicking in the Close box (the square in the dialog box's upper left-hand corner) you will add the directory-of-servers to your Sources window.

Searching the Directory-of-Servers

The directory-of-servers is an index of indexes. WAIS information providers are encouraged to register their sources with the

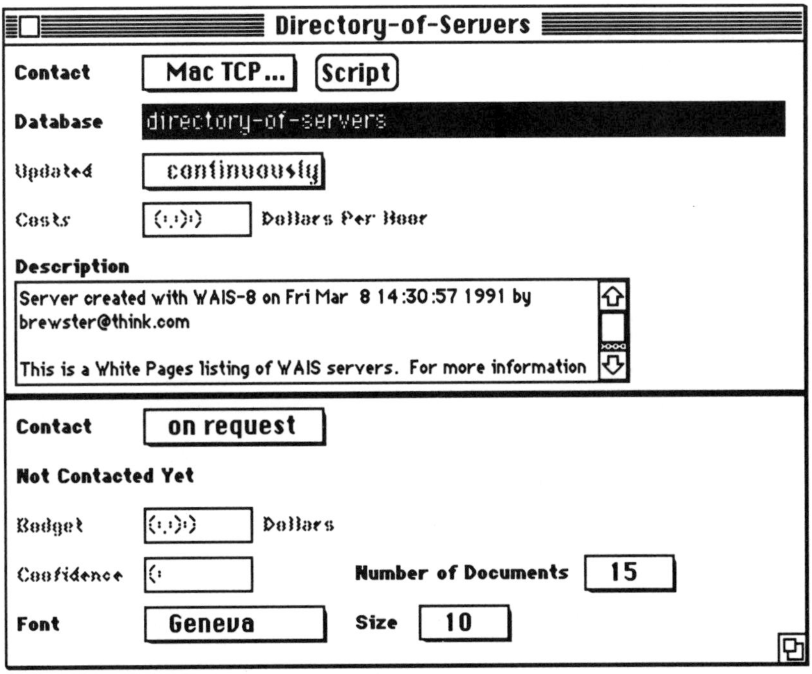

Figure 6-3. A listing of a source file (the directory-of-servers) in WAIStation.

directory-of-servers. Users, like yourself, can then search for other indexes in the hope of satisfying their information needs. An example will demonstrate this idea.

Suppose you wanted to find information dealing with astronomy. To locate WAIS sources on astronomy you can search the directory-of-servers for the word "astronomy":

1. Select New Question from the Question menu.
2. Enter the word "astronomy" into the field labeled "Look for documents about".
3. Drag the source, directory-of-servers, into the field labeled "In these sources".

Your window should look like the screen shown in Figure 6-4. Click the Run button.

At the bottom of the screen WAIStation will flash the progress of the search. In essence, WAIStation formulated a Z39.50-like query, opened a TCP/IP connection to a computer

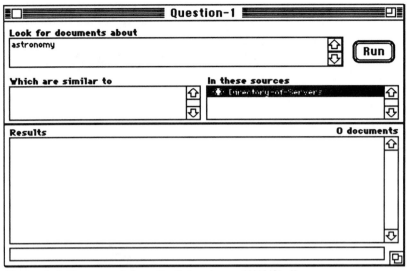

Figure 6-4. The search/results dialog box of WAIStation.

at Thinking Machines, sent the query, waited for a response from the directory-of-servers, retrieved the response, and displayed the results to you. Figure 6-5 presents the results.

Each one of the entries in the field labeled "Results" is a WAIS index whose description contains the word "astronomy."

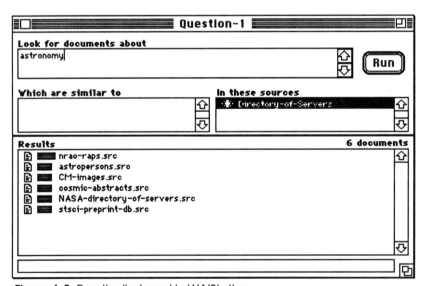

Figure 6-5. Results displayed in WAIStation.

Your success in retrieving results is based on the existence of a database on your topic, the terms you used to describe your information need, and the description of the databases written by the information provider.

Notice the horizontal bar in front of each item in the Results field. The length of this bar corresponds to the "relevance" of the located item. Therefore, based on the above example, the source "nrao-raps.src" is considered slightly more relevant than the source "astropersons.src".

You can view your results individually by double-clicking on them. WAIStation will retrieve the item from the database and display it. In this case you should see a dialog box very similar to the one describing the directory-of-servers (see Figure 6-3). Once displayed you can save the source information by selecting Save from the File menu. It is suggested you save all your sources in the Sources folder.

After you save the sources they appear in your Sources window (see Figure 6-7).

Take note of any sources that are named similarly to the directory-of-servers. One such source was located here, "NASA-directory-of-servers". As you might expect, this is another index of indexes and may point to other WAIS indexes dealing with

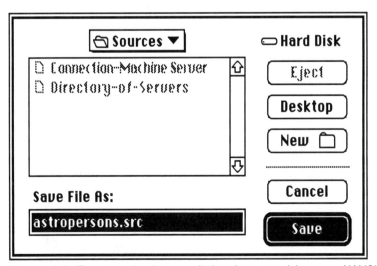

Figure 6-6. The standard save dialog box used to save WAIStation source files.

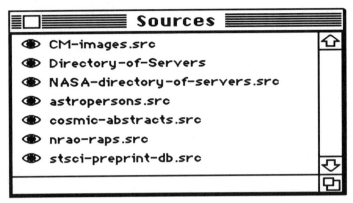

Figure 6-7. The Sources window after a few source files have been saved.

astronomy. A search of this database produces a list of a few more sources (see Figure 6-8).

Any directory-of-servers is good for locating other WAIS indexes, but you are not limited to the servers listed in these resources. Many times resources may not be listed in various directory-of-servers. In which case, you can create your own source file. To create your own source file you need to know three things:

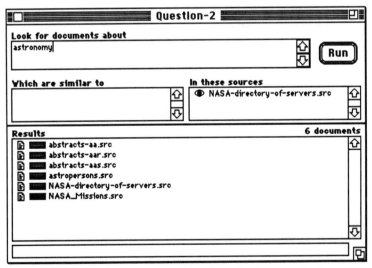

Figure 6-8. The results of search for the term "astronomy" using WAIStation.

1. the name or IP number of the computer hosting the database,
2. the port on the remote computer where searches are accepted, and
3. the name of the remote database.

For example, there is a WAIS index on dewey.lib.ncsu.edu called "Electronic Library Literature" (ell.src). This is an index of all the electronic serials whose subjects are library- and information-science related. Dewey.lib.ncsu.edu accepts WAIS queries on port 210, the standard Z39.50 port. Now select the Source/New Source menu option. The source dialog box appears. Begin by entering the name of the database in the database field. Next, if this database is a remote database, accessible through the Internet, then select MacTCP... from the Contact field. Now enter the name of the remote computer (dewey.lib.ncsu.edu) and the port (210). Close the dialog box and save the source information. The newly created source is now available for searching (see Figure 6-9).

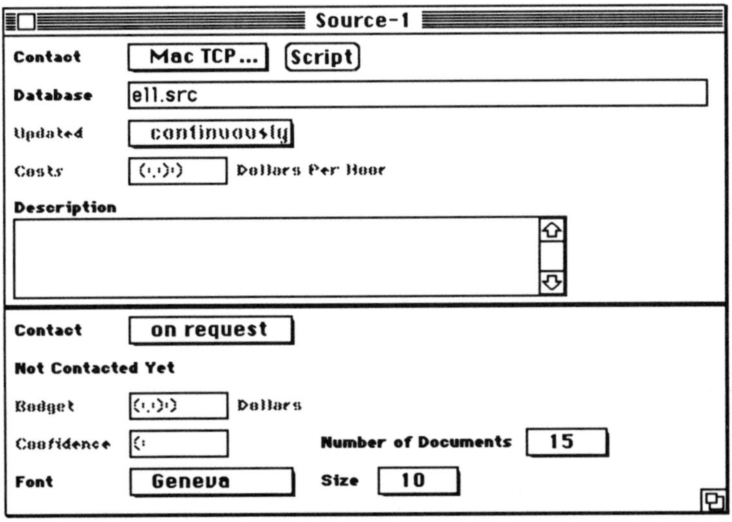

Figure 6-9. Creating source files with WAIStation.

Searching Other WAIS Indexes

Now, to find "real" information as opposed to meta-information, search the indexes you have identified for your chosen topic. In Figure 6-10, a search for "black holes" was applied to the indexes selected from the directory-of-servers.

As you can see, most of the items found from such a search resulted in citations containing the author's name "Black."

Scrolling down the list, one locates an item entitled "Evidence for Massive Black Holes in Galaxies." Opening that item (double-clicking on it) results in a citation from a book. In fact, most of the hits are citations from books. This shouldn't be surprising, since two of the sources are bibliographic databases.

WAIStation also supports a relevance feedback feature. This can be done in either of two ways. You can drag a source document into the "Which are similar to" field, or you can select some text from a document and add it to the "Which are similar to" window. Here is how to do this:

1. Open a document.
2. Select text (a paragraph) that is relevant to your query.
3. An icon of a few horizontal bars will appear.

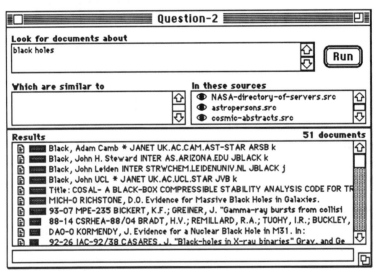

Figure 6-10. The results of the term "black holes" in sources located with the term "astronomy".

4. Drag the horizontal bars to the "Which are similar to" window.

5. Rerun your search by clicking the Run button.

Whichever of the two ways you choose, you click the Run button and your search will be repeated using the relevant text. After you follow this procedure your screen should look something like Figure 6-11.[3]

WAIS databases can contain things other than text. Although there are not many graphic databases available, the WAIStation program can deliver these items as well. Good examples can be found in the WAIS source "sample-pictures.src". A search for "africa" returns one item as shown in Figure 6-12.

Granted, this is not very useful, but it does demonstrate that graphics as well as text can be retrieved via WAIS clients.

After a question has been formulated, you can use WAIStation to save your questions. Simply select the File/Save...

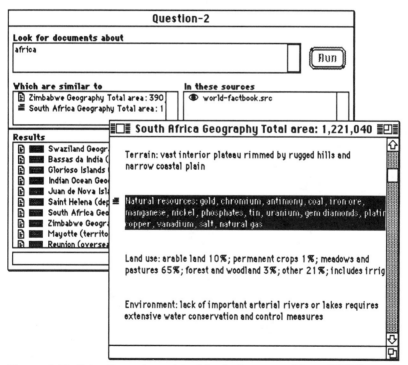

Figure 6-11. Selecting relevant text for further searching of WAIS sources.

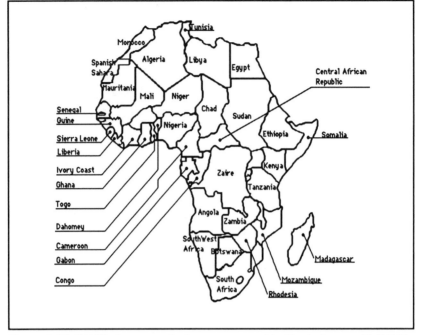

Figure 6-12. WAIStation can display some graphic files indexes with WAIS.

menu option. After a question has been saved it will appear in your Questions window. Double-clicking a question from the Questions window opens the question. You can now rerun the question by clicking the Run button. This feature is good if you run the same question over and over again on data that is constantly changing. Alternatively, you could run current awareness searches against a number of databases once a month (or every day or every week) if you desired.

Notes

1. URL=file://think.com/wais/wais-for-mac-1.1.sea.hqx or URL=file://dewey.lib.ncsu.edu/pub/stacks/finding/wais-for-mac-1.1.sea.hqx.
2. URL=file://mendel.welch.jhu.edu:/pub/fs/HyperWais.sea.hqx or URL=file://dewey.lib.ncsu.edu/pub/stacks/finding/HyperWais.sea.hqx.
3. This is a difficult process to demonstrate on paper. Consider viewing the WAIS Canned Demo by Steve Cisler. URL=file://dewey.lib.ncsu.edu/pub/stacks/finding/WAIStation-Canned-Demo.sit.hqx or URL=file://think.com/wais/WAIStation-Canned-Demo.sit.hqx.

7

TurboGopher, a Gopher
Client for the Macintosh

This chapter describes how to use the University of Minnesota's Gopher client, TurboGopher version 1.07.

TurboGopher is the only one of the three Gopher clients for the Macintosh that is also a Gopher+ client. Additionally, there are MacGopher[1] and GopherApp.[2] Both of these clients, as well as TurboGopher, can be downloaded from the Finding directory. Both MacGopher (by Rhett "Jonzy" Jones at the University of Utah) and GopherApp (by Don Gilbert at Indiana University) work; they do what they are supposed to do. Feel free to try them. They provide an excellent opportunity to examine how different programs can implement the same protocol.

TurboGopher, like the clients named above, requires MacTCP. MacTCP is a Macintosh operating system extension enabling your Macintosh to "speak" TCP/IP. MacTCP can be purchased from Apple computer.

When you launch TurboGopher for the first time, it randomly connects to the main "gopher hole" at gopher2.tc.umn.edu or gopher.tc.umn.edu. To change these settings and "point" your Gopher client to another server, use the Setup/Configure TurboGopher menu. For the purposes of this book, point TurboGopher to dewey.lib.ncsu.edu on port 70. This is the Gopher at the North Carolina State University Libraries. Now when you restart TurboGopher or choose Start Gopher from the File menu, your client connects to the designated server and a window appears as shown in Figure 7-1.

From here you simply double-click on the items in the window to navigate the server. You can use the arrow keys to select items. You can also type in letters from the beginning of menu items to go to those items. Press return to open the item.

Help in TurboGopher is available in three ways. First, there is Balloon Help.™ Balloon Help works only if you are using

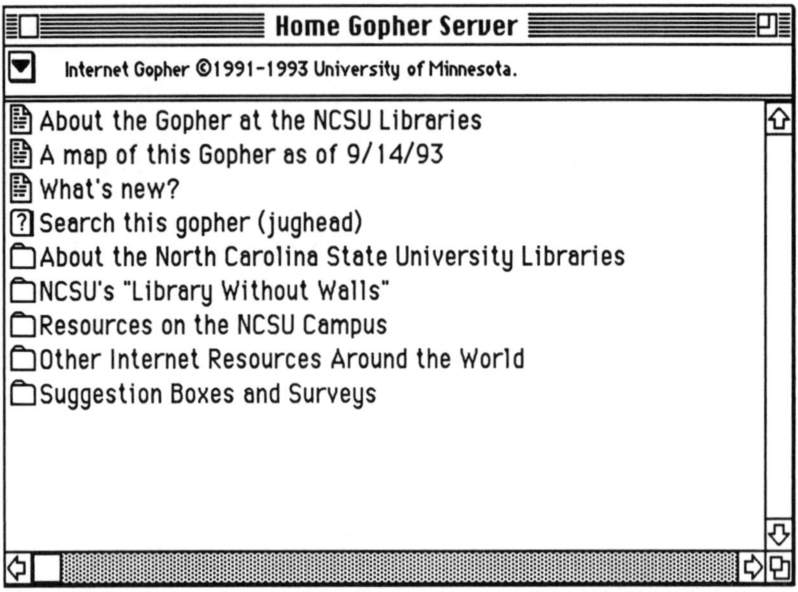

```
┌─────────────────────────────────────────────────────────────┐
│ ▤□▤▤▤▤▤▤▤▤▤▤▤▤▤▤ Home Gopher Server ▤▤▤▤▤▤▤▤▤▤▤ ▣▤ │
├─────────────────────────────────────────────────────────────┤
│ ▼   Internet Gopher ©1991-1993 University of Minnesota.       │
├─────────────────────────────────────────────────────────────┤
│ 📄 About the Gopher at the NCSU Libraries                 ⇧ │
│ 📄 A map of this Gopher as of 9/14/93                        │
│ 📄 What's new?                                               │
│ ❓ Search this gopher (jughead)                              │
│ 📁 About the North Carolina State University Libraries       │
│ 📁 NCSU's "Library Without Walls"                            │
│ 📁 Resources on the NCSU Campus                              │
│ 📁 Other Internet Resources Around the World                 │
│ 📁 Suggestion Boxes and Surveys                              │
│                                                              │
│                                                          ⇩ │
├─────────────────────────────────────────────────────────────┤
│ ◁ ▨▨▨▨▨▨▨▨▨▨▨▨▨▨▨▨▨▨▨▨▨▨▨▨▨▨▨▨▨▨▨▨▨▨▨▨ ▷▣ │
└─────────────────────────────────────────────────────────────┘
```

Figure 7-1. The main menu of the gopher at the NCSU Libraries using TurbGopher.

System 7. Select Show Balloons from the Balloon menu of the menu bar. Now point your cursor to features on the screen. A little cartoonlike balloon will appear briefly describing that item. Balloons are not available for items in the windows. Turn off the balloons by selecting Hide Balloons from the menu bar. The entire TurboGopher documentation is available from the menu as well. Choose Help from the Gopher menu. From here you can save the documentation by choosing Save As Text... from the File menu. Finally, for people who can't get enough, there is a document in the Finding folder called "inside TurboGopher".[3] This document describes a few of the more technical details of TurboGopher.

When using any Gopher client, menu items are marked with symbols representing types of items. TurboGopher is no exception. Figure 7-2 shows a list of the standard Gopher items and their symbols in TurboGopher.

Each of these items will be described below.

Text files are ASCII files. In our example, the "About the Gopher at the NCSU Libraries" item is a text file. When you select this menu item, TurboGopher retrieves the text file and displays it in a window (see Figure 7-3).

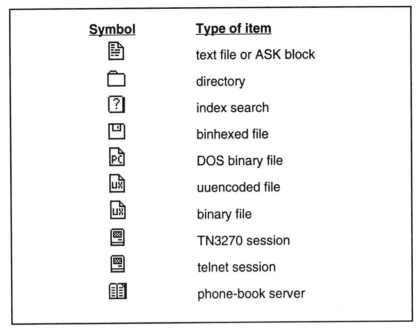

Figure 7-2. A list of standard gopher items and their symbols in TurboGopher.

From here you can cut, copy, and paste from the text to your heart's content. You can also save the text with the Save As Text... option from the File menu. Last, you can change the font of the text with the option under the Setup menu.

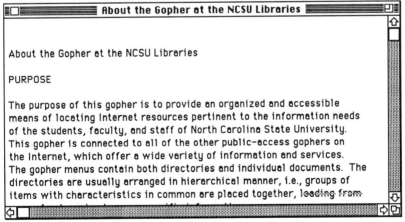

Figure 7-3. The display of a text file using TurboGopher.

Directories are containers of other menu items. By opening a directory you access more menu items. When you open the directory "NCSU's 'Library Without Walls'" you are presented with the screen shown in Figure 7-4.

If you hold down the Option key while opening a directory, then the new window will appear and the previous window will disappear. This makes your screen less cluttered. You can make this the default operation by selecting the "Single directory window" under the Setup/Options menu.

Now that you have opened a few windows, there are other ways to navigate Gopherspace with TurboGopher. First, you can use the Recent menu to open (or reopen) a window you have recently seen. You can also hold down the Command key and click on a window's title bar. You will then be presented with a pop-up menu of the path you took to get to this menu. You cannot select an item from the pop-up menu to return to that item.

Items with the question mark icons are index searches. Index searches can be links to WAIS indexes, veronica searches, or any other type of index someone might have created. Select "Search this gopher (jughead)" and you will be presented with a dialog box requesting you to supply terms to be searched (see Figure 7-5).

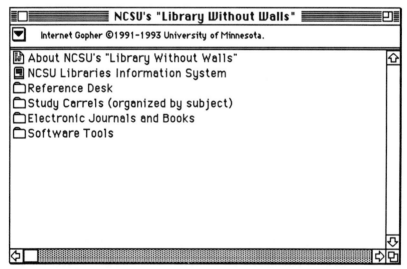

Figure 7-4. A submenu of the gopher at the NCSU Libraries.

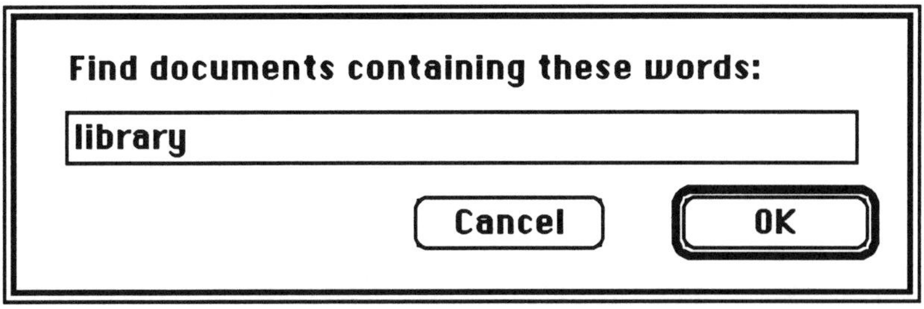

Find documents containing these words:

library

Cancel   OK

Figure 7-5. Searching indexes with TurboGopher.

This particular index search is a jughead search, a kind of mini-veronica (jughead indexes are described in more detail in chapter 10 of this book). Search for "library" (see Figure 7-6).

Notice that it returned items where the term "library" was contained anywhere within the menu item. Notice also that many different item types were returned: index searches, telnet sessions, text files, directories. You can now select any of these items and use them accordingly.

Another index type is the WAIS index type. In the "Stacks" is a collection of electronic journals. Using "Current Cites" as an example, you can search a WAIS index of all the back issues of

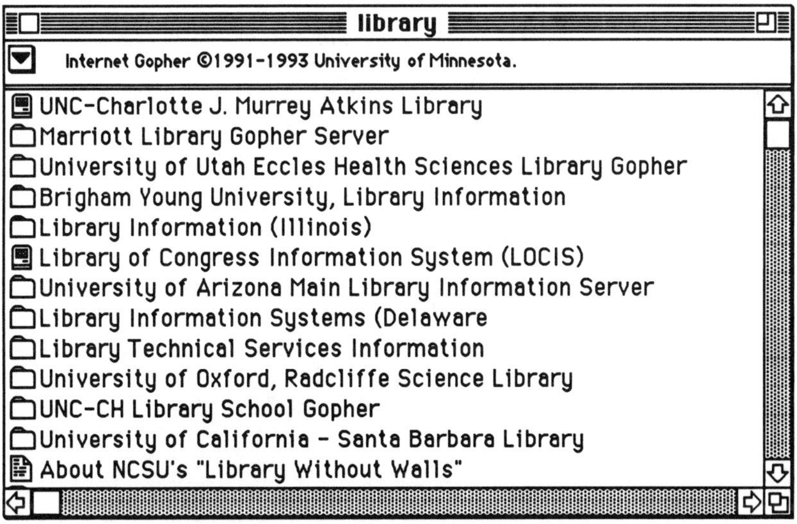

library

Internet Gopher ©1991–1993 University of Minnesota.

- UNC-Charlotte J. Murrey Atkins Library
- Marriott Library Gopher Server
- University of Utah Eccles Health Sciences Library Gopher
- Brigham Young University, Library Information
- Library Information (Illinois)
- Library of Congress Information System (LOCIS)
- University of Arizona Main Library Information Server
- Library Information Systems (Delaware
- Library Technical Services Information
- University of Oxford, Radcliffe Science Library
- UNC-CH Library School Gopher
- University of California – Santa Barbara Library
- About NCSU's "Library Without Walls"

Figure 7-6. The results of an index search.

Current Cites. A search for "senate" produces the results shown in Figure 7-7.

As before, you can now select any item from the retrieved list and view it. You can use the Find menu option under the Edit menu to locate the first occurrence of your search term in the displayed text.

WAIS indexes can take more than one term in the search query. Depending on the type of WAIS index it is, the queries can contain Boolean operators: and, or, not. To know which type of WAIS index you are searching you will have to rely on the description from the Gopher server administrator(s). Another but more difficult alternative is to locate the index with the WAIS client (as opposed to using WAIS through Gopher) and inspect the index's description.

There is a little-known pseudohypertext feature embedded in TurboGopher that comes in especially handy when searching WAIS indexes. After doing any sort of index search, hold down the Option key and double-click on a word of interest. This word will then be searched using the index you just used.

Menu items marked with a tiny disk icon are Macintosh binary files that have been binhexed, a form of translating the file into a text file for the purpose of transferring it over net-

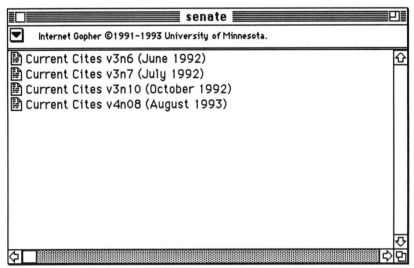

Figure 7-7. The results of a WAIS index search using TurboGopher.

works. To download one of these items, double-click it. TurboGopher will then ask you where you want to save the file and begin downloading it. During the transmission the Gopher cursor will run, and you can continue with your other work. When the file is completely transferred, you are given the opportunity to open the newly downloaded document.

Menu items represented by tiny PC or UX icons are DOS binary files or Unix binary files. If you download these files, they will not be of any use to you unless you copy them to a DOS or Unix computer.

Menu items with tiny Macintosh icons are remote login sessions: telnet or tn3270. For these menu items to work for you, you need the applications NCSA/BYU Telnet and/or tn3270, and you need them to be configured correctly. If you are using System 7 and you select one of these terminal sessions, TurboGopher first opens either the telnet program or tn3270, whichever is necessary. If you need a password to log on to the remote service, then TurboGopher will remind you of the password, as in the dialog box shown in Figure 7-8.

If no password is necessary, then the dialog box will not appear. On the other hand, if you are still running System 6, the TurboGopher will save a terminal session file on your hard disk. This file will contain the necessary information to connect to the remote service, but you will still have to remember the password. The moral of this story is "Upgrade to System 7."

Figure 7-8. TurboGopher reminds you of usernames for loging on to remote login services.

Finally, if the menu item is marked with a tiny telephone book icon, then the item is a CSO server. CSO servers are specialized databases of names, addresses, telephone numbers, and notes. When you select one of these items the following dialog box will appear (see Figure 7-9).

From here you can enter a search query, and the results will be returned to you. Alternatively, you can click the More Choices button and conduct a more specialized search (see Figure 7-10).

Using these pop-up menus and fields you can create a more specific search.

Bookmarks

After using Gopher for a while you will notice that you enjoy particular items and wish to return to them frequently. Navigating to these items can be trying, especially if they exist at the bottom of other menus. This is why TurboGopher supports bookmarks. Bookmarks are pointers to items in Gopherspace that you use frequently.

Here's how they work. Navigate Gopherspace and locate an item you find particularly appealing. Select it. Now select the Gopher/Set Bookmark... menu option. You will be prompted for a title for your bookmark. Enter one. Now a new window will appear with the title of the bookmark you just created. (If a new window does not appear, then select the Gopher/Show Bookmarks... menu item.) By selecting the title in the bookmark window you will navigate Gopherspace directly to that item. To add other items to your bookmark collection, simply repeat the process.

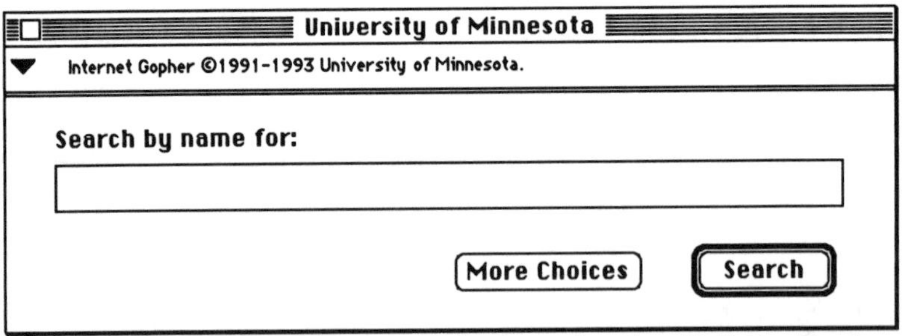

Figure 7-9. Simple searching of CSO phone books with TurboGopher.

```
┌─────────────────────────────────────────────────────────┐
│ ▤□ ═══════════ University of Minnesota 1 ════════════     │
│ ▼    Internet Gopher ©1991-1993 University of Minnesota.  │
│                                                           │
│  Directory Lookup                                         │
│ ┌───────────────────────────────────────────────────────┐│
│ │ Search the selected information source    ╭─────────╮  ││
│ │ using the criteria below:                 │ Search  │  ││
│ │                                           ╰─────────╯  ││
│ │ ┌──────────────┐  ┌──────────────┐ ┌────────────────┐ ││
│ │ │   name       │  │   equals     │ │                │ ││
│ │ └──────────────┘  └──────────────┘ └────────────────┘ ││
│ │ ☐ and                                                 ││
│ │ ┌──────────────┐  ┌──────────────┐ ┌────────────────┐ ││
│ │ │   name       │  │   equals     │ │                │ ││
│ │ └──────────────┘  └──────────────┘ └────────────────┘ ││
│ ├───────────────────────────────────────────────────────┤│
│ │ ◉ Return the default fields │✓ name              │ ⬆  ││
│ │                             │✓ alias             │    ││
│ │ ○ Return checked fields:    │✓ dn                │    ││
│ │                             │✓ email             │ ⬇  ││
│ └───────────────────────────────────────────────────────┘│
└─────────────────────────────────────────────────────────┘
```

Figure 7-10. More complex searching of CSO phone books servers with TurboGopher.

Any collection of bookmarks can be exported to a file with the File/Save as Bookmark File... option. If you have many files, then these files can be opened by TurboGopher and used. Here is how this function can be put to use. Collect items in Gopherspace concerning a particular subject and export them to a bookmark file. You can then give these bookmark files to other TurboGopher users, and they can benefit from your searching experience. GopherApp, another Macintosh Gopher client, handles this process more elegantly. With GopherApp you can not only save bookmarks but also specify the file where the bookmark is to be saved. This provides you with the opportunity to create your own, personalized view of Gopherspace, relieving you of having to rely on someone else's organization of information. Unfortunately, you cannot edit exported bookmark files with TurboGopher. Instead you must use some sort of text editor to manipulate the bookmark files. This is not a straightforward process.

ASK Blocks

ASK blocks are a feature the Gopher+ protocol. They appear as text items in your menus. They allow the server administrator to create electronic forms.

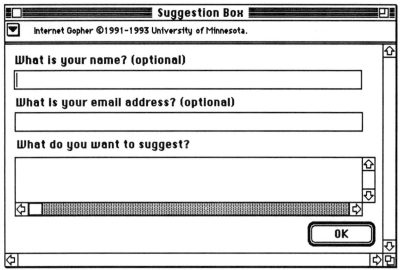

Figure 7-11. ASK blocks in TurboGopher.

Two examples of ASK blocks are located in "Suggestion Boxes and Surveys" of the Gopher at the NCSU Libraries. By selecting item 3, "Suggestion Box," the screen will appear as shown in Figure 7-11.

From here you can enter information into the fields and then click the "OK" button. Your responses will then be sent to the server and processed. The format of the ASK blocks and the processing done by the server is completely up to the server's administrator. (See chapter 10 for more information about ASK blocks.)

Notes

1. URL=file://ftp.cc.utah.edu/pub/gopher/Macintosh/MacGopher.sit.hqx or URL=file://dewey.lib.ncsu.edu/pub/stacks/finding/MacGopher.sit.hqx.
2. URL=file://ftp.bio.indiana.edu/util/gopher/gopherapp/gopherapp.hqx or URL=file://dewey.lib.ncsu.edu/pub/stacks/finding/gopherapp.hqx.
3. URL=file://dewey.lib.ncsu.edu/pub/stacks/finding/inside-TurboGopher.

8

Veronica: A Tool to Search Gopherspace

The number of Gopher servers in the world is increasing at a dramatic rate. Each of these servers contains a wealth of information. Because there are so many servers available, it becomes increasingly difficult to find the information you may need. This is why veronica was invented. Veronica is a tool used to search Gopherspace. The word "veronica" (always spelled with a lowercase v) is a cleverly elaborate acronym for Very Easy Rodent-Oriented Net-wide Index to Computerized Archives. Veronica was developed by Steve Foster and Fred Barrie at the University of Nevada.

There are two components of veronica, just as there are two components to WAIS: indexing and retrieval. As a user, you do not have to worry about the indexing, but this is how it works. About every two weeks the University of Nevada logs on and "walks" every publicly accessible Gopher server registered with the main Gopher server at the University of Minnesota. "Walking" a Gopher server means that every directory and directory item in a Gopher server is examined in terms of its title, attributes, location, and host. All this information is gathered and saved in a database. Duplicate items from the database are removed. Your veronica searches are then applied to this database.

The retrieval (searching) process begins by locating a link to a veronica server and issuing a query. (There is such a link in the Finding directory for your convenience.) After the query is processed, the results are sent back to your client, where you can select from the items as if they were any other Gopher item.

Veronica supports the following search features:

- Boolean searching,
- parenthetical statements,
- right truncation,

71

- limits by Gopher type, and
- limit the number of items retrieved.

Veronica searches can take the Boolean operators "and," "or," or "not" to improve precision and recall. Suppose there is a list of Gopher items each containing the term "ncsu." Suppose there was another list of Gopher items each containing the term "library." Using the Boolean operator "and" to combine the first term with the second produces a set representing the intersection of "ncsu" and "library." Conversely, combining the terms with a Boolean "or" produces a set representing the union of the two terms. Additionally, a Boolean "not" eliminates a term(s) from your query. Figures 8-1 through 8-3 illustrate these points.

Note that terms combined with neither "and" nor "or" default to "and."

Putting our example to work produces the following results:

Query	Number of hits
ncsu	106
library	4907
ncsu and library	2
ncsu library	2
ncsu or library	5013

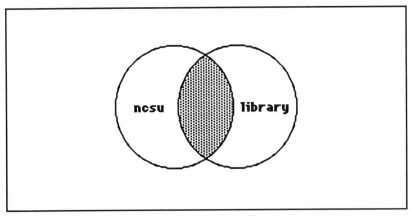

Figure 8-1. An illustration of a Boolean "and".

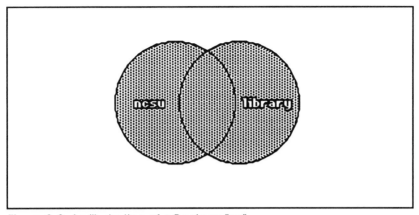

Figure 8-2. An illustration of a Boolean "or".

You can also use parentheses to qualify your searches. Consequently, veronica searches such as:

```
(ncsu or North Carolina State University) and library
```

are valid. Items within the parentheses will be processed before items outside the parentheses.

Veronica also allows stemming or right truncation. By appending an asterisk to a word, veronica will search for every variation of that word beginning with the letters you specified.

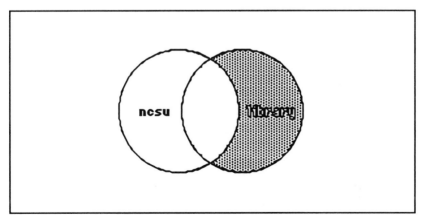

Figure 8-3. An illustration of a Boolean "not".

Therefore, the query

```
librar*
```

will return items including

- library,
- libraries,
- librarian,
- librarianship,

and so forth.

You can further limit your veronica searches by Gopher item type. This is done by placing a -t followed by one or more type specifiers anywhere in the search statement. You can list more than one specifier. For example, -t8 specifies telnet sessions; -t0 specifies text files; -t80 specifies telnet sessions or text files. Here is a list of the standard specifiers:

Gopher type	Specifier
text file	0
directory	1
CSO name server	2
Macintosh BinHex File	4
DOS binary file	5
Index	7
Telnet session	8
TN3270 session	T
Unix binary file	9

No more than one limiter is allowed per search statement and no spaces are allowed. Thus, the search statement "-t045 myers briggs" returns a list of Gopher items containing the words "myers" and "briggs" that are text files, Macintosh BinHex files, or DOS binary files.

There is even more power to veronica searches. You can limit the number of items returned with the -m parameter. veronica defaults to a limit of 200 items, but you can specify more or less than this number with a qualifier such as -m10 or -m1000.

One of the niftiest options is -l (dash lowercase L). This option allows you to return a link file containing all the items found from your search. This is very handy for Gopher administrators, since they can save this link file and put it into their own servers.

Finally, you can specify all or none of these qualifiers in your veronica queries. You just can't specify them more than once, and you can't combine them into a single qualifier. For example, the following query is valid:

```
((red or green) and blue) not black -t01 -l -m10
```

This query will return no more than 10 Gopher text files or directories as well as a link file that does not contain the word black, but does contain the word "blue" and the words "red or green."

9
Creating Servers

This chapter provides an outline of how to get your own WAIS and Gopher servers up and running. Please note that only an outline can be provided, primarily because everybody's situation is different.

The Hardware

This chapter will describe how to implement WAIS and Gopher servers on a Unix computer. I've chosen Unix for my example because WAIS and Gopher were designed on Unix computers, and therefore it is easier to get them working on Unix computers. (An added benefit of using Unix is the built-in TCP/IP capabilities of the Unix operating system.) Your computer should be equipped with a large hard disk. Eight hundred (800) MB or more is not unreasonable, because Unix takes up a very large portion of that space. Not including your Internet connection, a computer like this will cost in the ballpark of $5,000. Once your hardware is purchased and it is connected to the Internet, staff time will be the only costs you will incur. Finally, it will be very important for you to have root privileges on this computer, since you will need the authority to edit vital system configuration files.[1]

Creating a WAIS Server

To create a WAIS server, first retrieve the WAIS distribution.[2] This is a freeWAIS distribution, and it is described here because it offers significant enhancements to the original distribution.

You will now have to uncompress the archive with this command:

```
uncompress freeWAIS-0.1.tar.Z
```

You will then have to untar the archive with this command:

```
tar -xf freeWAIS-0.1.tar
```

The result will be the creation of a new directory (freeWAIS-0.1) containing all the things you need to create a freeWAIS server except your data. Change directories to freeWAIS-0.1 and read the README file. It will give you an idea of things to come.

Next you will edit the file named "Makefile." This file contains parameters needed to compile the distribution. Read the comments in Makefile and follow the instructions. At the very least you will have to edit line 48. This line defines where your WAIS distribution source file is located. If you are unsure about what else to edit, then don't edit anything but line 48.

Compile the distribution with the command "make."

After about five minutes of processing, your WAIS distribution should be compiled. Don't worry unduly if the compilation process returns warnings. You need only be concerned if the compilation process exits before it makes the server or the indexer. Read the output from the compilation process to see if it got this far. If it didn't, then try editing other options in Makefile or post a query to the USENET newsgroup comp.infosystems.wais or consult your nearest Unix guru.

The result of the compilation process is a number of binaries:

- swais — the curses WAIS client described in chapter 4
- waissearch — a command line WAIS client
- waisserver — the server
- waisindex — the indexer

You can check to see whether the clients work by running them. The WAIS distributions come with some sample sources for this purpose.

Your next step will be to index some data with waisindex. To make life simple, begin by indexing some textual data. An output of the complete description of the waisindex command can be retrieved by entering waisindex at the prompt without any parameters, but here is the format as presented in the man page:

```
waisindex [ -d index_filename ] [ -a ] [ -r ]
[ -mem mbytes ] [ -register ] [ -t type ] [ -export ]
[ -nocat ] filename
```

Here is one example of how to use waisindex:

```
waisindex -d /usr/indexes/alawon.src -t first_line\
-export /usr/data/alawon
```

where

- -d /usr/indexes/alawon.src is the index to be created,
- -t first_line specifies that the data is text and the first line of the file will be returned in the search results,
- -export specifies that the database will be available via the Internet, and
- /usr/data/alawon is the directory/file to be indexed (your data).

Other useful options include

- -r to recursively index all the data in the specified directory,
- -register to register this database with the directory-of-servers,
- -t text for indexing simple text files, and
- -t filename where text files are indexed but their filenames are returned.

After you have indexed some data you will want to test your server. To do this you need to run the server program. The server command, waisserver, takes the following form:

```
waisserver [ -p [ port_number ] ] [ -s ] [ -d\
directory ] [ -e [ path-name ] ] [ -l log_level ]\
[-u user ] [ -v ]
```

Therefore, the waisserver command

```
waisserver -p 210 -d /usr/indexes/
```

establishes a WAIS server on port 210 and will look for databases in the /usr/indexes directory.

Once you have indexed some data and you are running the server, check to make sure it works by using one of the clients you have just compiled. (Remember, if you want to use the swais client, then you will have to have saved your index in the directory specified by the swais.sh file. Otherwise, you may want to use the waissearch client instead.)

If things don't work, then try again making sure your data was indexed correctly and you specified the options for the waisserver properly.

Last, after you have gotten everything working correctly, you will want to make sure the waisserver is always available. The most efficient way to do this is to run the waisserver under inetd. Inetd is the Internet daemon. Read the man pages for more information about inetd or consult the books referenced earlier in the chapter.

To run waisserver under inetd you will have to edit vital system configuration files. For example, if your Unix computer is BSD-like, then you will edit the /etc/services and /etc/inetd.conf files. Add the following line to /etc/services:

```
z3950 210/tcp # WAIS
```

This specifies that connections to port 210 to your machine will be used for Z39.50 connections. (Actually, this is a bit misleading because the freeWAIS distribution implements only a shadow of the Z39.50 standard.)

Next, add a line to your /etc/inetd.conf file to specify the program to run (waissearch) when a connection is made on port 210:

```
z3950 stream tcp nowait /usr/bin/waisserver\
waisserver.d -d /usr/indexes -e /usr/bin/wais.log -l 5
```

This entry in your inetd.conf file is only an example. Again, consult your man pages because your particular circumstances may call for something different.

Last, kill inetd and restart it with the command /etc/inetd. Your computer should now be "listening" on port 210 for connections and sending any requests on that port to the WAIS server.

Creating a Gopher Server

Creating a Gopher server is much like creating a WAIS server. First you will retrieve the necessary files, compile the software, make sure it works, and install it under inetd.

Begin by retrieving the server archive.[3] The Gopher server software, as well as the client software, is being enhanced all the time. This chapter will describe how to install version 2.08.

Next, uncompress the archive:

```
uncompress gopher2.08.tar.Z
```

and then untar it:

```
tar -xf gopher2.08.tar.Z
```

The result will be a new directory named Gopher 2.08 containing everything you need to make a Gopher server.

The Gopher 2.08/doc directory contains the Gopher documentation. Specifically you will want to read the INSTALL file. It outlines the compilation process. Additional documentation can be found in the *Internet User's Gopher Guide.*[4]

If you want to compile into your Gopher server the ability to search WAIS indexes, then you will first have to compile a WAIS distribution and symbolically link the WAIS resource libraries to the Gopher source directory. This is done from the Gopher 2.08 directory by entering the following commands:

```
ln -s waistop/ir .
ln -s waistop/bin .
ln -s waistop/ui .
```

where waistop is the top level directory of your WAIS distribution.

Next, edit the Makefile.conf file. This file is used by the "make" command to compile the distribution. The comments in Makefile.conf are straightforward. You will have to specify such things as:

- what compiler you are using,
- where your files are to be installed,
- where the Gopher data directory begins,
- your domain or domain name, and
- what port your server will use for communications.

As with the WAIS distribution, don't worry if you don't know all the answers to all the questions. For the most part, the default entries will work just fine. After editing Makefile.conf you will want to edit the conf.h file. One of the most important things in this file is the name of the computer that your Gopher client will point to by default. Also, at the very end of the file you will want to specify the future location of a file called gopherd.conf. Gopherd.conf specifies characteristics of your Gopher server and its contents. The other parameters in conf.h are used to specify other server behaviors. Experiment with them after you have gotten the server working for a little while.

After you have finished editing Makefile.conf and conf.h, enter the command "make" and the computer should do the rest. If things don't work, then simply try something else or consult the experts in the USENET newsgroup comp.infosystems.gopher.

Once a server has been compiled, it is time to test it out. Create a directory that will contain the data you intend to serve. In that directory put any text file. Now start up the server. The Gopher server command "gopherd" takes the following form:

```
gopherd [-DIc][-o optionfile] [-L loadavg]\
[-1 logfile] [-u userid] [-U uid] datadir port
```

For testing purposes try this variation:

```
gopherd /usr/indexes 70
```

where /usr/indexes is the directory containing your data (specified in Makefile.conf), and 70 is the port the server will listen to for connections.

Now simply telnet on port 70 to the computer hosting the server. Once connected, press return. Before the server automatically closes the connection, a selector string representing each of the items in the specified directory should be returned. If this happens then you are in business. For a better test, try pointing your favorite Gopher client to your server and see what happens.

The next step is to run gopherd under inetd. This is the most efficient means of running the Gopher server because gopherd will become active only when there is a connection. Otherwise it will lie dormant and take up many processing cycles. To run gopherd under inetd you must edit vital system configuration files. These files will be different on different implementations of Unix, so consult the man pages for inetd.

To run gopherd under inetd on a BSD-like Unix computer, you will have to edit the /etc/services and /etc/inetd.conf files. Put the following line in /etc/services:

```
gopher 70/tcp # gopher
```

This specifies to the computer to run the Gopher program listed in the inetd.conf file when a connection is made on port 70.

Next, put something like the following line in your /etc/inetd.conf file to ensure that your server will be running whenever you reboot the computer and to eliminate the need to have the server always in RAM except when called upon:

```
Gopher stream tcp nowait /usr/gopher/bin/gopherd\
gopherd -I -cC
```

You will now have to kill inetd and restart it so it recognizes the new entry.

Last, you will want to edit your gopherd.conf file. This file specifies more information about your server. First of all, it should be located in the directory you said it was going to be located in from your conf.h file. Second, the sample conf.h file will work as is with only a minor modification. All you have to do is edit the name and address of the Gopher server administrator. Finally, since records in your inetd.conf file take only a limited number of fields, you can add a line like this in your gopherd.conf file:

```
Logfile: /usr/users/temp/gopher/bin/gopher.log
```

This will specify that a log of gopher server transactions will be kept in a file named gopher.log of the /usr/users/temp/gopher/bin directory.

Create an Organizational Scheme

Now that you have the hardware and software up and running, it is time to sit back, relax, pat yourself on the back for your recent accomplishments, and think about how you are going to organize your data. It does not matter what your organizational scheme is as long as it is consistent and recognizable to your users. The Gopher at the NCSU Libraries uses a library model. For example, there is the Reference Desk. In this section of the server there are links to information you would find at a reference desk: dictionaries, thesauri, names, telephone numbers, addresses ("snailmail" and e-mail), and indexes.

The Discipline Specific Study Carrels represent our classification scheme. Here we have put other Internet resources (ftp sites, telnet sites, WAIS indexes, etexts, etc.) that are of particular interest to specific segments of the NCSU students, faculty, and staff. We decided that when the number of Internet resources of a particular discipline reaches a critical mass of four items, it is time to create a new study carrel. Presently our study carrels include Agriculture and Biology, Astronomy and Astrophysics, Chemistry, Computer Science, Earth Science, Economics, Education, Fine Arts, Government and Law, History, Library and Information Science, Literature and Journalism, Mathematics, Medicine, Physics, Religious and Philosophical Studies, and Sociology and Psychology.

Since libraries are in the business of providing information, we thought it would be appropriate to provide a section for software whose primary purpose is to gather information. Consequently, there is the Software Tools for Gathering Information section. It contains Gopher, ftp, and USENET clients, as well as miscellaneous programs for DOS, Windows, and Macintosh computers.

Finally, there is the Stacks. The Stacks is where all the full-text information is located. This includes ejournals, links to

Project Gutenberg or the Online Book Initiative, and many other full-text resources, such as the complete works of Shakespeare, the Declaration of Independence, and the World Factbook.

Note that any resource from the four sections listed above (Reference Desk, Study Carrels, Software Tools, and the Stacks) can also be put in another section. Unlike physical information resources (books and journals), these electronic tools can be located in more than one place without duplicating resources.

If you are setting up a server for a college department, you may want to set up a section for each different subject according to your particular environment. If you are in a business, then you might want to organize your information according to your departments. Again, it doesn't matter what organizational scheme you use just as long as it is consistent and recognizable.

By making directories and .cap files you can implement your organizational scheme. Your Gopher server will initially point to a data directory. Under that directory will be other directories implementing your structure. To enhance the titles your users see when accessing your server, you can use .cap files.[5] These are two-line text files residing is directories named ".cap". These two-line text files are abbreviated .link files. (See "Collect Your Data," later in this chapter, for an explanation of link files.)

For example, you might have a directory structure under your Gopher server's Gopher data directory that looks like this:

```
/usr/gopher/data/
    .cap/
        reference
        stacks
        disciplines
    reference/
        .cap/
          guides
          indexes
          directories
        guides/
        indexes/
        directories/
    stacks/
        alice.txt
        bible.txt
        shakespeare.txt
```

```
disciplines/
   .cap/
     agriculture
     medicine
     economics
     physics
   agriculture/
   medicine/
   economics/
   physics/
```

Notice the directories; notice how there are files within the .cap directories with the same names as the directories. The file "agriculture" in the /usr/gopher/data/disciplines/.cap directory may look like this:

```
Name=Agriculture Resources
Type=1
```

When your users access the /usr/gopher/data/disciplines directory, the Gopher server will read the entries in the .cap directory and display "Agriculture Resources" to the user.

In short, use .cap files to present to the user meaningful Gopher title names.

Collect Your Data

Now the fun begins; it is time to fill your server. Listen to the Internet. Seek out and find Internet resources pertinent to your institution. Then create link files to point the users of your Gopher to those resources. Link files are five- or six-line text files placed in your Gopher server's data directory. They contain all the necessary information for your Gopher client to transport you to an ftp site, search a WAIS index, telnet to an OPAC, or display a graphic. Below is a link file to the NCSU Libraries Information System:

```
Name=NCSU Libraries Information System
Type=8
Port=23
Path=LIBRARY
Host=library.ncsu.edu
```

The first line lists what the user of your server will see. The second line lists the kind of resource this is. (An "8" means a telnet session.) The Port line tells you the port where the TCP/IP communications will take place. In this case, the Path line lists the password needed to log on to the system, "LIBRARY". Last, the Host line gives you the Internet address of the resource.

It is easy to create these link files. Just use your Gopher curses client to explore other people's servers. When you find a resource you like, press the equals (=) key and that resource's link file will be displayed. Now you can copy and paste the displayed text into your text editor. Instant link files.

Some link files are better created by hand. Link files to WAIS indexes are a good example. If you want to provide WAIS searching through your Gopher server, then you need to first put the WAIS source files in a directory below the Gopher server's data directory, and you need to create a link file for that index. The link file will look something like this:

```
Name=Search ALAWON
Type=7
Port=70
Path=waissrc:/.wais/alawon.src
Host=dewey.lib.ncsu.edu
```

This is just like any other link file except for the Path line. The waissrc: part of the line specifies that this item is a WAIS search. The /.wais/ specifies the directory under the Gopher data directory where the WAIS source file resides. The alawon.src is the WAIS source file used to make the connections to the remote WAIS server.

Keep in mind, this is not the only way to put WAIS searches in your Gopher server. The Gopher distributions after version 1.12 provide the capability to simply drop a source file into a Gopher data directory. The source file will work, but it won't have a very pretty name. Furthermore, this method does not allow you to specify where in the Users menu the item will appear, because it will appear alphabetically.

Remote ftp sites are done similarly. Below is a link file to 'Sumex, an ftp archive of Macintosh software:

```
Name=ftp to 'Sumex, an ftp archive of Macintosh software
Numb=2
Type=1
Port=70
Path=ftp:sumex-aim.stanford.edu@/pub/info-mac/
Host=dewey.lib.ncsu.edu
```

Here the Path line specifies that the resource is an ftp site. The server specified in the Host line is to open an ftp connection to sumex-aim.stanford.edu, change directories to pub/info-mac, and display the files listed there.

This can be the technique used when you save electronic texts in your own ftp archive. Instead of specifying a Type of 1 (directory), you will want to specify a Type of 0 (file). Then the Path line would not only specify the computer with the archive, but it would also specify the full path name of the remote file:

```
Name=ALAWON v2n26 (June 21, 1993)
Type=0
Port=70
Path=ftp:dewey.lib.ncsu.edu@/pub/stacks/alawon/alawon-v2n26
Host=dewey.lib.ncsu.edu
```

After you have begun collecting your data, especially your full-text data, you will be able to provide access to it in three ways: ftp, Gopher, and WAIS. You can provide these services with only one copy of the data. If you do, then your information system will be set up as Figure 9-1 illustrates.

Conclusion

Bringing up WAIS and Gopher servers is not too difficult. It requires perseverance and the willingness to learn new technologies. The instructions that come with the distributions, the instructions laid out here, and the help of others on the Internet provide all the assistance you will need to get started. Once you have brought your server(s) up, your work has just begun. You will want to maintain your server by removing old information and updating new information. You will want to listen to the Internet for new developments and improvements. Think of it as a challenge.

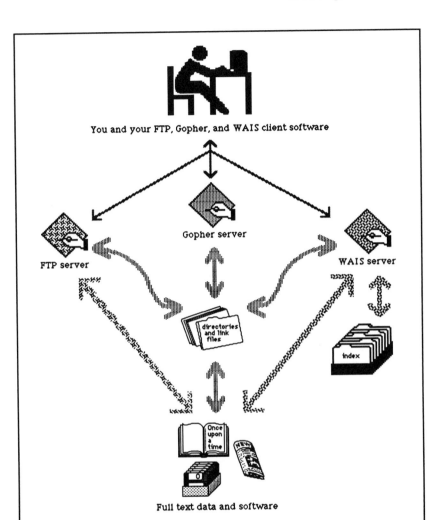

You and your FTP, Gopher, and WAIS client software

Gopher server

FTP server

WAIS server

directories
and link
files

index

Once
upon
a
time

NEWS

Full text data and software

Figure 9-1. An illustration depicting the relationship of users, clients, servers, and data.

The WAIS, ftp, and Gopher protocols are powerful tools for retrieving, organizing, storing, and disseminating information, but be forewarned. Computer technology is constantly changing, and these protocols will be superseded sometime in the future. On the other hand, the institutions that actively explore the use of these services will be that much ahead of the game when the new technologies emerge. "Go-fer it!"

Notes

1. If you are new to Unix, then you may want to read up on the Unix operating system. There is a plethora of titles available. If you are new to Unix systems administration, then these three titles may be of interest: E. Nemeth, *UNIX® System Administration Handbook* (Englewood Cliffs, NJ: Prentice Hall, 1989); A. E. Frisch, *Essential System Administration* (Sebastopol, CA: O'Reilly, 1991); and C. Hunt, *TCP/IP Network Administration* (Sebastopol, CA: O'Reilly, 1992). I have found all of these sources indispensable.
2. URL=file:://dewey.lib.ncsu.edu/pub/stacks/finding/ freeWAIS-0.1.tar.Z or URL=file:://ftp.cnidr.org/pub/NIDR.tools/freeWAIS-0.1.tar.Z.
3. URL=file://dewey.lib.ncsu.edu/pub/stacks/finding/gopher2.08.tar.Z or URL=file://boombox.micro.umn.edu/pub/gopher/Unix/gopher2.08.tar.Z.
4. URL=file://dewey.lib.ncsu.edu/pub/stacks/finding/GopherGuide_Jun15b.txt; URL=file://dewey.lib.ncsu.edu/pub/stacks/finding/GopherGuide_Jun15b.ps; URL=file://boombox.micro.umn.edu/pub/gopher/docs/GopherGuide_Jun1 5b.ps; or URL=file://boombox.micro.umn.edu/pub/gopher/docs/Gopher Guide_Jun15b.txt.
5. Newer versions of the Gopher server software use .name file instead of .cap directories. You have your choice of either of these options in your Makefile.conf file. While both work, .cap files are a bit harder to maintain. There have been some difficulties with .name files.

10
Server Tools

This chapter describes some tools you can use on your Gopher server to enhance service and analyze performance. It does not list all the server tools available, just a few that are particularly noteworthy.

Perl

The quintessential tool is a scripting language called perl.[1] Make no bones about it, perl is a programming language, and none of the tools mentioned in this chapter works without perl.

Perl was written by Larry Wall, and he has coauthored a book entitled *Programming perl*. It is an excellent book, very readable, by far the most enjoyable manual ever written. The book has instructions for compiling the perl distribution.

Go4gw

Go4gw is a program that comes with the Gopher distribution. It allows you to add additional services to your Gopher server such as USENET News, whois, archie, specialized ftp searches, or things like the Geographic Name Server. (Ftp used to be implemented through Go4gw, but a few versions ago ftp became a built-in feature of the server.) To add these extra services to your server you must install the gateways. There are a number of them that come with the distribution, and the documentation describes how to get them up and running.

Jughead

Jughead[2] provides a way to index your Gopher server. Jughead stands for Jonzy's Universal Gopher Hierarchy Excavation And Display. It was written by Rhett "Jonzy" Jones of the University of Utah.

As the jughead's man page states:

Jughead is used to excavate through Gopher menus, display the hierarchy of the encountered menus, acquire the name of the hosts accessed via a given server, build search tables, or run as a search engine waiting to do boolean searches on menu titles. The purpose of this program is to give a linear view of a Gopher hierarchy, or allow users to search through menu titles of a given Gopher server or group of Gopher servers, where the boolean operators AND, OR, and NOT are supported as well as partial word searches.

To install jughead you first uncompress and untar the archive. Then you edit the file Makefile for your site. Next you create a data file containing the items in your server:

```
jughead -tm -b jughead.dat -X "ftp:*"\
dewey.lib.ncsu.edu
```

Then you build an index and hash table of your data for improved performance:

```
jughead -B jughead.dat
```

Last, you run jughead as a server application:

```
jughead -S -l jughead.log -u Eric jughead.dat
```

Jughead is elegant and fast, and since it supports Boolean operators and truncation you can narrow your searches quite nicely.

Gmail

Gmail,[3] as described by its author, Prentice Riddle of Rice University, is a mail-to-Gopherspace interface and events calendar. With gmail a person can send an e-mail message to a Unix account, and the message will be saved in an administrator-defined Gopher data directory. This is a handy tool if you need many people adding information to your Gopher server. A limiting factor of gmail is its inability to have more than one directory specified for a single user.

Newitems

A script by Dennis Boone, newitems[4] "generates a link file listing all items in a Gopher tree modified in the last n days." Since the output file consists of link files, this file can be put into other data directories or edited to display user-friendly menu items.

GopherReport and gla

GopherReport and gla analyze your Gopher log file and create an output listing

- the number of connections to your server
- the domains connecting to your server
- the entries which are most popular
- errors

GopherReport[5] was written by Eric Katz at the National Center for Supercomputing Applications (NCSA). Its nice feature is the ability to produce graphs. Below is a sample output from GopherReport. This particular output shows the days of the week that the server is used the most for a particular domain, *.com:

```
                    Connections Per Weekday
     Day            Connections
     -----------------------------------------------------------
     Sunday        1   ***
     Monday        9   ******************************************
     Tuesday       7   ********************************
     Wednesday     5   ***********************
     Thursday      8   ***********************************
     Friday        7   ********************************
     Saturday

     Total for this Section: 37
```

It is obvious from this report that commercial organizations do not use the server on Saturday and very little on Sunday.

Dennis Boone's gla[6] (Gopher log analyzer) produces reports listing the computers connecting to your server as well as the files they were accessing. Gla can also rank these listings according to use. Here is a small sample of the output from gla. It lists the top users and most popular sections of the Gopher at the NCSU Libraries:

Michigan State University Gopher Log Analyzer   Page: 1
                Client Domains by Frequency of Use

Host Domain or IP Address	Calls	%	Cum
ohiolink.edu	69516	14.5	14.5
lib.ncsu.edu	27739	5.8	20.3
u.washington.edu	22104	4.6	24.9
com	8896	1.9	26.8
ucsd.edu	8350	1.7	28.5
hh.lib.umich.edu	7661	1.6	30.1
uc.wlu.edu	7090	1.5	31.6
loc.gov	6119	1.3	32.9
uoregon.edu	5490	1.1	34.1
micro.umn.edu	5399	1.1	35.2
ces.ncsu.edu	4979	1.0	36.2
cc.ncsu.edu	4472	0.9	37.2

.
.
.

Michigan State University Gopher Log Analyzer Page: 1
Retrieved Items by Frequency of Use

File Description	Uses	%	Cum
/library	40617	8.5	8.5
/library/disciplines	25329	5.3	13.8
Root Connection	25159	5.3	19.0
/library/reference/guides	23353	4.9	23.9
/library/stacks	18410	3.8	27.8
/library/reference	18403	3.8	31.6
/library/about	8041	1.7	33.3
/library/software	7455	1.6	34.8
/beyond	6714	1.4	36.2
/library/stacks/acadlist	6271	1.3	37.6
/beyond/bbs	6064	1.3	38.8
/beyond/bbs/cleveland	5772	1.2	40.0
/library/disciplines/library	5693	1.2	41.2
/library/disciplines/history/ archives	5562	1.2	42.4

```
/library/reference/indexes          5228    1.1    43.5
/library/reference/dictionaries     4774    1.0    44.5
/library/disciplines/government     4759    1.0    45.5
/library/disciplines/arts/music     4508    0.9    46.4
/library/reference/directories      4312    0.9    47.3
/library/disciplines/literature     4277    0.9    48.2
/library/reference/directories/
   addresses                        4176    0.9    49.1
/beyond/ftp                         4112    0.9    49.9
```

ASK Blocks

Since the introduction of Gopher, the University of Minnesota Gopher Team has enhanced the protocol. The newer protocol is called Gopher+. One of the features of Gopher+ is ASK blocks. ASK blocks provide the server administrator with the ability to query the user, process the user's response(s), and act on the response(s).With this capability, a Gopher server administrator can create forms to be completed, e-mail messages to be sent, or specialized database queries to be processed. The administrator is limited only by his or her imagination and his or her ability to write a program to process the ASK block results.

To get this to work you need to write two text files. The first file contains the ASK block. The second file processes the responses from the user. The first file must have the same name as the second file, except that it includes .ask as its suffix. For example, you might have suggestion.ask and suggestion, where suggestion.ask contains the ASK information and suggestion processes the ASK block responses.

An ASK block consists of a number of expressions in which the first term on each line is one of the following commands:

- Ask
- AskP
- AskL
- AskF
- Select
- Choose
- ChooseF
- Note

Each of these commands is followed by a colon (:). Choose and Select are further followed by a string of characters and a tab-delimited list of choices, whereas the rest of the commands are followed only by a string of characters.

According to the Gopher+ protocol,[7] this is what each command is suppose to do:

- "Ask" presents the user with a question, supplies a default text answer if it exists, and allows the user to enter a one-line response.
- "AskP" presents the user with a question and bullets out the response typed in by the user so that someone watching over the user's shoulder cannot read the response.
- "AskL" presents the user with a question and ideally should allow the user to enter several lines of response.
- "AskF" requests the user for a new local filename, presumably for stashing the response returned by the server. It may supply a default filename.
- "Select" presents the user with a set of options from which the user can select one or many. This is equivalent to Macintosh check boxes.
- "Choose" presents the user with a few short choices, only one of which may be selected at a time. This is equivalent to Macintosh radio buttons.
- "ChooseF" requests that the user select an existing local file, presumably for sending to the server. On some systems, the client writer or administrator might want to restrict the selection of such files to the current directory (i.e., not allow paths in the filename to prevent sending things like password files).

Unfortunately, developers (server administrators) have not been able to get all of these commands to work, specifically ChooseF and AskF. Similarly, for a user to successfully use these items, the user must be using a Gopher+ client. (All the client programs described in this book are Gopher+ clients except PC

Gopher III.) Even then, not all Gopher+ clients work quite right or present the information to the user in a "pretty" form.

Despite these difficulties, ASK blocks do work. Here is a simple ASK block used as a suggestion box:

```
Ask:    What is your name? (optional)
Ask:    What is your email address? (optional)
Note:   What do you want to suggest?
AskL:
```

Here is an ASK block used as a rudimentary survey:

```
Note:   Please take a minute to answer
Note:   a few questions about your use
Note:   of the Gopher at the NCSU Libraries.
Note:   Where are you located?
Choose: Location Off campus On campus
Note:   What is the operating system of your
Note:   primary Gopher client?
Choose: Operating System Macintosh DOS Windows Unix
Note:   Which section of the Gopher at the
Note:   NCSU Libraries do you use the most?
Choose: Section 'On campus 'Beyond campus Reference Desk
Note:   How would you classify yourself?
Choose: Classification Undergraduate Graduate Staff
Ask:    What is your name? (optional)
Ask:    What is your email address? (optional)
Note:   If you have anything to add,
Note:   then please feel free to do it here.
AskL:
```

Each ASK block file must have an accompanying file to process the response(s). This file can be any sort of shell or perl script, or a compiled program.[8] Here is the file suggestion. It is the csh script used to process the results from suggestion.ask:

```
#!/bin/csh -b

# create an address to send the suggestion
set suggestionbox = eric_morgan@ncsu.edu

# create a variable for the text of the message
set tmpfile = /tmp/gomf$$
```

```
# get the first parts of the input from the ASK block
set name = $<
set address = $<
set nlines = $<

# remove bogus characters from the address
set address = `echo $address|tr -cd '[^A-Za-z0-1@._-\
    +=#&:;,~]' `

# create the temporary text file
touch $tmpfile

# add an email header to the text file
echo "Subject: *** Suggestion ***" >> $tmpfile
echo "Reply-To: $address" >> $tmpfile
echo "From: $name <$address>" >> $tmpfile
echo "X-Mailer: Gopher <Eric@minerva.lib.ncsu.edu>" >>\
    $tmpfile
echo "" >> $tmpfile

# get the rest of the text from the ASK block
set i = 0
while ($i < $nlines)
 set text = $<
 echo $text >> $tmpfile
 @ i++
end

# mail the text
/usr/lib/sendmail -ba $suggestionbox < $tmpfile
```

Here is the shell script processing survey.ask:

```
#!/bin/csh -b

# create an address to send the results
set surveybox = eric_morgan@ncsu.edu

# create a variable for the text of the message
set tmpfile = /tmp/gomf$$

# get the location
set location = $<

# what OS do they use
set operatingSystem = $<
```

```
# what section do they like
set section = $<

# what type of person are they
set classification = $<

# get their name
set name = $<

# get their address
set address = $<

# remove bogus characters from the address
set address = `echo $address|tr -cd '[^A-Za-z0-1@._-\
    +=#&:;,~]' `

# get the number of lines in any comment they made
set nlines = $<

# create the temporary text file
touch $tmpfile

# append an email header to the text file
echo "Subject: *** Survey ***" >> $tmpfile
echo "Reply-To: $address" >> $tmpfile
echo "From: $name <$address>" >> $tmpfile
echo "X-Mailer: Gopher <Eric@minerva.lib.ncsu.edu>" >>\
    $tmpfile
echo "" >> $tmpfile

# append the answers to the text file
echo $location >> $tmpfile
echo $operatingSystem >> $tmpfile
echo $section >> $tmpfile
echo $classification >> $tmpfile

# get the balance of the user's input; get the comment
set i = 0
while ($i < $nlines)
 set comment = $<
 echo $comment >> $tmpfile
 @ i++
end

# mail the text
/usr/lib/sendmail -ba $surveybox < $tmpfile
```

```
# delete the text
/bin/rm $tmpfile

# report to the user what happened
echo "Thank you for completing the survey."
echo "Your responses have been sent to\
    eric_morgan@ncsu.edu."
```

In both cases, the scripts first read a set number of variables based on the user's input. Second, they build an e-mail message including the user's responses. Third, they deliver the e-mail message, and last, they delete a temporary file and report back to the user what has happened.

ASK blocks create all sorts of exciting possibilities. Experiment.

Alcuin for Organizing WAIS Indexes

There exist more than 400 publicly available WAIS indexes around the world. (A list of these indexes can be ftp'ed from think.com.) Besides figuring out how WAIS searching is done, a Gopher administrator is concerned with organizing and managing a collection of WAIS indexes. With the Gopher protocol it is easy to put a front end on WAIS, but the matters of organization and management still exist. This is where Alcuin[9] comes in. Alcuin is a perl script written by the author and used to organize WAIS indexes in a Gopher server's data directory.

This is how Alcuin works. First you ftp the list of publicly available WAIS indexes from think.com. Then uncompress and untar the archive.

Second, configure Alcuin so it knows where your data files reside. Do this by editing the file al.

Third, put Alcuin to work. Alcuin reads the list of WAIS indexes and puts the list into an array (new list). Alcuin then reads a list of the WAIS indexes you already own (old list). It then subtracts the old list from the new list. Next, Alcuin reads the list of WAIS indexes you don't want in your Gopher server and puts that into an array (trash list), and Alcuin subtracts the trash list from the new list. The final list contains items that are new to the server. The initialization process is complete after Alcuin creates a directory-tree listing of your Gopher server.

Last, Alcuin presents you with a menu similar to the one below:

```
There are 356 new items remaining.
The next item is ANU-Pacific-Manuscripts.src.
What do you want to do?

   (V)iew it   (E)valuate it
   (S)kip it   (A)dd it
   (T)rash it

   (L)ist the remaining items
   List the (O)ld items
   List the t(R)ash items

   (Q)uit

   (V, E, S, A, L, O, T, R, or Q) ==>>
```

This is what the choices do:

```
Choice  Action
   V    displays the .src file with the "more" command
   E    runs the waissearch program
   S    goes to the next item
   A    prompts for a cool name for the index,
        displays Gopher server's directory tree,
        prompts for a directory,
        saves a link file in the specified directory, and
        optionally saves the link file in other directories
   L    lists the remaining new items
   O    lists the old items
   T    adds the .src file to the trash list
   R    lists the trashed items
   Q    quits
```

Depending on your menu selection(s), Alcuin cycles through the list of new WAIS indexes until each one has been processed. Then, about once a week, you can download the list of WAIS indexes from Thinking Machines and start the whole process over again. Granted, the first time through you have many items to inspect, but after that the job gets easier.

Alcuin makes a number of assumptions. First, it assumes that all your WAIS indexes are located in one directory within your Gopher server's data directory. Second, it assumes you have the waissearch binary that came with the Thinking Machines WAIS distribution. Third, Alcuin assumes you use a terminal with a large scroll-back buffer, because the Gopher tree listing and output from waissearch can be many, many screens long.

Notes

1. URL=file://dewey.lib.ncsu.edu/pub/stacks/finding/perl-4.036.tar.gz or URL=file://prep.ai.mit.edu/pub/gnu/perl-4.036.tar.gz. These archives are compressed with a GNU compression program, gzip. You will need this program to uncompress perl. URL=file://dewey.lib.ncsu.edu/pub/stacks/finding/gzip-1.2.2.shar or URL=file://prep.ai.mit.edu/pub/gnu/gzip-1.2.2.shar.
2. URL=file://dewey.lib.ncsu.edu/pub/stacks/finding/jughead.0.9.tar.Z or URL=file://boombox.micro.umn.edu/pub/gopher/Unix/GopherTools/jughead/jughead.0.9.tar.Z.
3. URL=file://dewey.lib.ncsu.edu/pub/stacks/finding/gmail.shar.
4. URL=file://dewey.lib.ncsu.edu/pub/stacks/finding/newitems.
5. URL=file://dewey.lib.ncsu.edu/pub/stacks/finding/GopherReport.
6. URL=file://dewey.lib.ncsu.edu/pub/stacks/finding/gla.
7. URL=file://dewey.lib.ncsu.edu/pub/stacks/finding/gopher+.txt or URL=file://boombox.micro.umn.edu/pub/gopher/gopher_protocol/Gopher+/Gopher+.txt.
8. No question about it, this part of the procedure is programming.
9. Alcuin is the name of a librarian from the Middle Ages. He was an advisor to Charlemagne, set up a school and a couple of libraries, studied the seven liberal arts, and wrote extensively on the subjects of rhetoric, logic, and dialectic. I figured his name would be good for a program that systematically collects and manages WAIS indexes. URL=file://dewey.lib.ncsu.edu/pub/stacks/finding/al.

11

Gopher, WAIS, Ftp, and Electronic Serials

This book has so far described how to set up WAIS and Gopher servers. Now this knowledge will be applied to the systematic collection of electronic journals and newsletters. This chapter describes one way to create a working collection of electronic journals.

To date there are hundreds of electronic serials as listed in the *Directory of Electronic Journals and Newsletters.*[1] The vast majority of these serials are newsletters as opposed to journals; most of the serials do not go through a peer review process. Despite this fact, you may want to collect many of these serials.

There are a number of problems that come to mind when you begin a collection of electronic serials. What serials do you want to collect? Since most of the serials are available through some sort of listserv, how do you handle all the mail that will arrive in your electronic mailbox? How do you process each new issue once it arrives? How do you handle missing issues? How do you provide access to the serial? Can you index the serial so it can be searched? How do you do all this and continue your day-to-day responsibilities? In other words, before you begin subscribing to electronic serials, you need to know;

- where you are going to save them,
- how you are going to organize them,
- how you are going to provide access to them, and
- how you are going to process them once they arrive.

One answer to these questions is to use WAIS, Gopher, ftp, procmail, and the perl script called "ac."

Deciding which serials to collect is something this book can't help you do. This sort of decision depends on your collection development policy.

Ftp for Storage and Rudimentary Access

Using ftp is a straightforward way of storing (archiving) electronic serials and providing rudimentary access to them. This way anybody can get the articles if they have full access to the Internet.

The method for creating an anonymous ftp archive depends on your computer's operating system. I suggest you use some sort of Unix computer because the WAIS indexer works best on Unix computers. Consult your particular Unix computer's man pages for instructions on setting up an anonymous ftp server.[2]

Within your anonymous ftp server's directory, create a single directory for each title. Within that directory plan to save all the issues and articles from that title, each with a unique identifying name. Take Citations for Serial Literature (CSL) as an example. Every issue of CSL could be designated to begin with a serial code such as "csl". Since CSL is issued in volume and number, each designation could be followed with something like "-v1n22". Therefore a complete name for an issue of CSL could be "csl-v1n22". Similarly, issues from Public Access Computer Systems News would be "pacsn-v1n03". IR List Digest, which comes out sequentially, could be saved as "irld-001". Take note of the leading zeros in the preceding examples. The zeros make it possible to sort the files accurately by volume and number, and consequently date. Keep in mind that the serial codes you create can be completely arbitrary. As long as the codes are consistent, then it doesn't matter what they are.

Gopher for Simplified Access and Organization

Ftp is strong on storage but weak on access. This is where a Gopher comes in. The Gopher protocol excels at maintaining pointers to Internet resources. Since anonymous ftp sites are Internet resources, and since you have a Gopher server in place, you can create Gopher pointers (link files) to your collection of electronic serials. This solves a number of problems. First, the link files provide the capability to list files in a more readable fashion. Second, the user no longer has to use ftp commands to access the collection. Below is a link file from the collection of electronic serials in the Gopher at the NCSU Libraries:

```
Name=ALAWON v2n18 (May 10, 1993)
Type=0
Port=70
Path=ftp:dewey.lib.ncsu.edu@/pub/stacks/alawon/alawon-v2n18
Host=dewey.lib.ncsu.edu
```

When the patron uses the Gopher he or she sees "ALA-WON v1n35 (May 5, 1992)." When the item is selected the Gopher transparently opens up an anonymous ftp connection to dewey.lib.ncsu.edu, changes to the /pub/stacks/alawon directory, retrieves the file "alawon-v1n35" as a text (ASCII) file, closes the connection, and sends the text back to your client software, where it is displayed. From there you can save the file on your local computer.

Furthermore, the Gopher protocol allows you to organize your serials into volumes or years with an abbreviated link file called a ".cap" file. Thus you can organize your collection and eliminate very long menu listings. For example, suppose you have a Gopher directory named alawon. ALAWON is now into volume 2. Therefore you might want to create two subdirectories of alawon. One could be named v1 and the other could be named v2. Then, in your .cap directory, one link file named v1 would look like this:

```
Name=Volume 1 (1992)
Type=1
```

The other link file, v2, would look like this:

```
Name=Volume 2 (1993)
Type=1
```

Then each directory (v1 and v2) is where you will store the link files that point to your ftp archive and the text itself (see Figure 11-1).

WAIS for Enhanced (Keyword) Access

You are now using ftp primarily for storage and rudimentary access. With Gopher you simplified access and organized the information. Unfortunately ftp and Gopher are useful only if

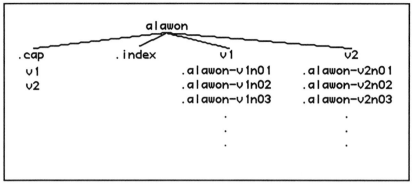

Figure 11-1. A directory structure displaying the relationship of .cap, and link files in gopher server data directory.

the patron knows exactly which issue or article they want. WAIS now enters the picture, allowing the patron to search your collection via keywords.

Since you own all the articles associated with any particular electronic serial, and since you have a WAIS server in place, then it is a simple matter of creating a WAIS index for each of your titles and putting these indexes in the appropriate directory of the Gopher server. This can be done with a shell script. Below is part of the script used to index the titles on dewey.lib.ncsu.edu:

```
# usage: index <leaf name>
#
# index ALAWON
cd /usr/users/Eric/wais/bin
set wi=/usr/users/Eric/wais/bin/waisindex
if "$1" == "alawon" then
    set theIndex=/usr/users/temp/gopher/data/.wais/$1
    set theDirectory=/usr/users/temp/ftp/pub/stacks/$1\
$wi -d $theIndex -r -t first_line -export
    $theDirectory
exit
endif
```

The script is called "index." It take one argument, the serial code representing a title to be indexed. The script first changes to the directory where the WAIS indexer is saved. It then creates a variable containing the full path name of the WAIS indexer. Then, if the argument from the command line equals "alawon," it creates a variable called "theIndex" containing the full path name of the to-be-created index. It then creates another variable, "theDirectory," containing the full path name of the location of the data to be indexed. Finally, the shell script runs the WAIS indexer and indexes the data. In this case, the data is indexed with the -r, -t first_line, and -export options. The option -r tells the WAIS indexer to index recursively through the directory. The option -t first_line tells the WAIS indexer that each file's first line will be the headline. Finally, -export tells the WAIS indexer that this index will be available over the Internet. A complete version of this shell script is available in the Finding directory.[3]

Once your WAIS index is created you will want to create a link to it with a link file (.index) such as the following:

```
Name=Search ALAWON
Type=7
Port=70
Path=waissrc:/.wais/alawon.src
Host=dewey.lib.ncsu.edu
```

One obvious place you will want to put such a link file is one directory higher than the link files pointing to your data. (See Figure 11-1.)

An exciting proposition presents itself when you start to collect more than one serial title in the same subject area: subject indexes. For example, if you collected all the electronic serials that dealt with library and information science, then, in addition to indexing individual titles, you could also index the entire set of serials. In other words, you would first index one title. Then you would index another title but append the indexing of the second title to the indexing of the first title. You then continue this process until all your titles have been indexed.

Again, a shell script is all that is needed. Here is another section of the index shell script that indexes a complete collection of the library and information science electronic serials:

```
# now the moment you've all been waiting for... create
# the "Electronic Library Literature Index"
if "$1" == "ell" then
  set theIndex=/usr/users/temp/gopher/data/.wais/ell
  set theDirectory=/usr/users/temp/ftp/pub/stacks/acq
```

```
    $wi -d $theIndex -r -t first_line -export $theDirectory
    set theDirectory=/usr/users/temp/ftp/pub/stacks/alawon
    $wi -d $theIndex -r -a -t first_line -export $theDirectory
    set theDirectory=/usr/users/temp/ftp/pub/stacks/nnews
    $wi -d $theIndex -r -a -t first_line -export $theDirectory
    set theDirectory=/usr/users/temp/ftp/pub/stacks/currentc
    $wi -d $theIndex -r -a -t first_line -export $theDirectory
    set theDirectory=/usr/users/temp/ftp/pub/stacks/irld
    $wi -d $theIndex -r -a -t first_line -export $theDirectory
    set theDirectory=/usr/users/temp/ftp/pub/stacks/pacsr
    $wi -d $theIndex -r -a -t filename -export $theDirectory
    set theDirectory=/usr/users/temp/ftp/pub/stacks/prices
    $wi -d $theIndex -r -a -t first_line -export $theDirectory
    set theDirectory=/usr/users/temp/ftp/pub/stacks/pacsn
    $wi -d $theIndex -r -a -t filename -export $theDirectory
    set theDirectory=/usr/users/temp/ftp/pub/stacks/csl
    $wi -d $theIndex -r -a -t first_line -export $theDirectory
    set theDirectory=/usr/users/temp/ftp/pub/stacks/lccn
    $wi -d $theIndex -r -a -t first_line -export $theDirectory
    set theDirectory=/usr/users/temp/ftp/pub/stacks/ann
    $wi -d $theIndex -r -a -t filename -export $theDirectory
    set theDirectory=/usr/users/temp/ftp/pub/stacks/libres
    $wi -d $theIndex -r -a -t first_line -export $theDirectory
    set theDirectory=/usr/users/temp/ftp/pub/stacks/sts
    $wi -d $theIndex -r -a -t first_line -export $theDirectory
    set theDirectory=/usr/users/temp/ftp/pub/stacks/mcj
    $wi -d $theIndex -r -a -t first_line -export $theDirectory
  exit
  endif
```

You will notice that this section of the shell script looks exactly like the previous section except for two differences. First, in this section, more than one title is being indexed into "theIndex," and second, the -a option was applied for all iterations of the WAIS indexer except for the first iteration. The -a option causes the indexing to be appended to the previous indexing.

There are at least two caveats to indexing your serials. The first regards disk space. Presently, the entire ALAWON collection of one and a half years takes up 376,665 bytes (.4 MB) of disk space, but the index takes 756,309 bytes (.8 MB). The indexing takes up almost twice as much space as the original data. This is not a problem at the moment since the data and indexing amount to only a little over 1 MB of data. On the other hand, in a few years, after continuous collection, disk space may become a problem. Obviously, the larger your hard disk capacity, the better off you will be in the long run. The problem is compounded when a subject index is created!

Another problem of indexing your serials is time. Using a fairly fast workstation (a DECstation 5000), the time it takes to reindex the entire collection is well over 30 minutes. In a year the indexing process may take more than an hour. To reduce the effect of this problem you can set up an entry in your crontab file to have your data reindexed on a regular basis while no one else is using the computer. (Cron is a Unix command that issues other commands at specified times. Crontab is a list of the commands to execute. Again, refer to the man pages of your Unix computer for more information.) This is the entry in the crontab file on dewey.lib.ncsu that handles reindexing:

```
30 2 * * * csh /usr/users/Eric/wais/bin/index all
```

This entry means that every day at 2:30 A.M. the computer will execute the C shell script /usr/users/Eric/wais/bin/index all. Thus, everything gets reindexed automatically while the computer is generally not being used for other purposes.

Collecting Back Issues

After all this planning (the creation of an ftp server, an organizational scheme in a Gopher server, and a way to search your data), you are ready for the really good stuff, actually collecting the titles.

The sooner you get started, the better off you will be. This is because the number of electronic serials is only going to increase, and since the vast majority of these serials are free, there is no excuse for not having a complete collection.

Most electronic serials are distributed through a listserv program. Some electronic serials are also archived at ftp sites. In either case, you will want to begin by retrieving all the back issues. If the serial is distributed via a listserv program, then begin by sending the listserv the "index" command. In return you will get a list of all the files available for the specified listserv.

Next, using the "get" command, retrieve individual files, not log files. Individual files will be easier to process. This may take a couple of days because listserv generally does not allow you to retrieve more than a set number of files or bytes per day. (You can get around this problem if you work as a team with other people who are collecting different issues from the same list.) As the issues arrive, save them in a directory for later processing.

Similarly, if the serial is archived at an ftp site, then use your ftp client's version of the "get" command to retrieve the back files. Again, save these files in a directory for later processing.

Now you need to do two things: massage your data and create link files.

Massaging your data is optional. It means removing any header information from the text. It may also mean prefixing the text with some sort of identifying information like the human name of the text and a computer name of the file. For example, you may want to remove the header and replace it with something like the following:

```
ALAWON v2n20 (May 21, 1993)
File: alawon-v2n20
```

The advantage of this comes into play when the user retrieves and saves or prints the document, which now has an intelligible source reference in addition to its Filename.

Creating link files can be a bit more tedious. One option is to

1. move your edited issues to the ftp directory,
2. create a link to that directory within your Gopher server,
3. run the Gopher curses client,
4. navigate to the link you just created,
5. capture link files from each issue with the "=" key,
6. edit the captured link files, and
7. save the edited link files in your Gopher directory.

This is the brute-force method and is not recommended.

Another method is to use a Gopher tool named "newitems."[4] This perl script, written by Dennis Boone of Michigan State University, points to a directory, reads its contents based on the date, and outputs a file containing links to items in the directory. After using newitems it will be up to you to edit the output file, give the links human-understandable titles, and save the file in your appropriate Gopher directory.

Using Procmail and "Ac" to Automate Acquisitions

The process described above requires no programming experience, except for the shell scripts. It does require the judicious use of an ftp client, a Gopher client, and an text editor.

Using procmail and a perl script called "ac" you can automate much of the process outlined above, if you are willing to learn a bit of programing.

Procmail[5] is a mail-processing program written by Stephen R. van den Berg. As it's readme file states, procmail can be used to "create mail-servers, mailing lists, sort your incoming mail into separate folders/files, preprocess your mail, start any programs upon mail arrival or selectively forward certain incoming mail automatically to someone." You will want to explore procmail's capability to sort your incoming mail into separate folders and files.

A copy of the procmail archive has been saved in the Finding folder. The latest version of procmail can be ftp'ed from amaru.informatik.rwth-aachen.de, but use archie to find a copy closer to home.

After you compile and install procmail, you create "recipes" in a .procmailrc file. The .procmailrc file specifies how procmail will process your incoming mail. You will want to save incoming mail from listservs with unique but consistently named files for later processing. Here is a part of a .procmailrc file:

```
# process mail from ALAWON
MSGPREFIX=ala
:c:
^From.*ALA-WO@UICVM.BITNET
/usr/users/MrSerial/process-us
        :a
        |(echo "Mail from ALAWON";formail -x Subject:)\
        | mail Eric_morgan@ncsu.edu
```

In short, this is how it works. When new mail arrives, the

mail gets forwarded to procmail. Procmail first defines a prefix (ala) for all subsequent file names. Procmail reads the From line of the header. If the header contains "ALA-WO@UICVM.BIT-NET", then procmail knows this message is from ALAWON. Procmail saves the mail message in a user-specified directory (/usr/users/MrSerial/process-us). Then procmail sends a message to someone notifying them of the arrival of new mail.

You create a recipe in your .procmailrc file for each serial to which you subscribe. This enables you to sort and save all your serials for processing with ac, which is described below.

You use ac[6] (a perl script written by the author) to process the newly arrived issues. "Ac" is short for "acquisitions." Here is the algorithm for ac:

1. locate an e-mail message,
2. remove the header,
3. prepend the name of the file to the message,
4. save the file in the ftp directory,
5. create and save a Gopher link file,
6. delete the original e-mail message, and
7. "cook until done" (repeat).

The heart and power of ac lie in steps 3 and 5 because this is where elements of a serial's issue are automatically extracted to create an ftp name and Gopher link file. For example, the following code fragment extracts the month from an issue of ALA-WON:

```
$theMonth = &getword (1, @theText[$fl + 9]);
```

It just so happens that the month is the first word of line nine after the header. Similarly, the day is the second word of line nine:

```
$theDay = &getword (2, @theText[$fl + 9]);
```

Once all the necessary elements (day, month, year, issue number) are extracted, they are concatenated with predefined Unix path names to create ftp filenames and Gopher link files:

```
Name=ALAWON v2n10 (March 24, 1993)
```

```
Type=0
Port=70
Path=ftp:dewey.lib.ncsu.edu@/pub/stacks/alawon/alawon-v2n10
Host=dewey.lib.ncsu.edu
```

Next, the issue's email header is replaced with a meaningful title such as ALAWON v2n10 (March 24, 1993) and an ftp name, alawon-v2n10.

Finally, the "marked" issue is "shelved" in its ftp directory, and its Gopher link file is added to our Gopher directory (catalog).

There are a few problems with ac. First, it assumes that the necessary elements to create ftp filenames and Gopher link files are in the same place in every issue. This is not the case. If the format of the electronic journal is not consistent, then ac creates meaningless filenames and link files.

Second, perl scripting (programming) skills are necessary in order to modify ac or add a new serial to the collection. There is at least one solution to this problem, configuration files. Configuration files could be written with any text editor and they could be written in English. Then, when an issue is read, its corresponding configuration file is read, in turn, defining how to parse the issue. With such a scheme, there could be one perl script and many companion configuration files, one for each serial.

Summary

This chapter has presented one way to systematically collect electronic journals. Ftp is used to store the issues. Gopher is used to provide access. WAIS is used to search the collection. Procmail is used to preprocess each issue as it arrives. Ac is used to process each issue into the collection.

There are number of problems with the system. First, it supposes the electronic serials are initially delivered via e-mail. Second, it is limited to use on a Unix computer, since WAIS indexing is supported only on the Unix platform. Third, since new journals will be created all the time and present journals are not consistently formatted, perl scripting ability is necessary to maintain ac. Fourth, this system does not address the problem of bibliographic control, nor holding statements.

On the other hand, with this system an individual can single-handed maintain a vast collection of electronic journals easily, efficiently, and in a timely manner.

Notes

1. URL=file://dewey.lib.ncsu.edu/pub/stacks/finding/ejournals.txt or send the following commands as an e-mail message to listserv@uottawa or listserv@acadvm1.uottawa.ca.
2. If you are new to Unix, then you may want to read up on the Unix operating system. There is a plethora of titles available. If you are new to Unix systems administration, then these three titles may be of interest: E. Nemeth, *UNIX® System Administration Handbook* (Englewood Cliffs, NJ: Prentice Hall, 1989); A. E. Frisch, *Essential System Administration* (Sebastopol, CA: O'Reilly, 1991); and C. Hunt, *TCP/IP Network Administration* (Sebastopol, CA: O'Reilly, 1992). I have found all of these sources indispensable.
3. URL=file://dewey.lib.ncsu.edu/pub/stacks/finding/index.sh.
4. URL=file://dewey.lib.ncsu.edu/pub/stacks/finding/newitems.
5. URL=file://ftp.informatik.rwth-aachen.de/pub/unix/procmail.tar.Z or URL=file://dewey.lib.ncsu.edu/pub/stacks/finding/procmail.tar.Z.
6. URL=file://dewey.lib.ncsu.edu/pub/stacks/finding/ac.

Index